$2.75

NEW LIFE FOR OLD BUILDINGS

EDITED BY

MILDRED F. SCHMERTZ, FAIA
EXECUTIVE EDITOR, ARCHITECTURAL RECORD

NEW LIFE FOR OLD BUILDINGS

AN ARCHITECTURAL RECORD BOOK

McGRAW-HILL BOOK COMPANY

NEW YORK
ST. LOUIS
SAN FRANCISCO
AUCKLAND
BOGOTA
HAMBURG
JOHANNESBURG
LONDON
MADRID
MEXICO
MONTREAL
NEW DELHI
PANAMA
PARIS
SAO PAULO
SINGAPORE
SYDNEY
TOKYO
TORONTO

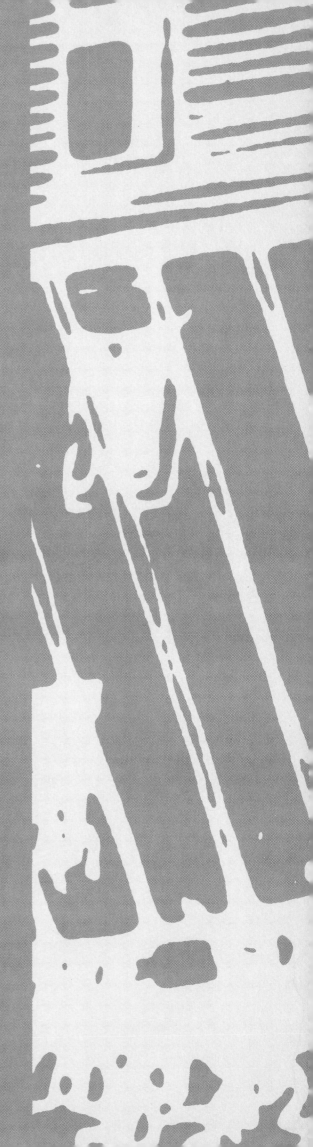

ARCHITECTURAL RECORD BOOKS

Affordable Houses
Apartments, Townhouses and Condominiums, 3/e
Architecture 1970-1980: A Decade of Change
The Architectural Record Book of Vacation Houses, 2/e
Buildings for Commerce and Industry
Buildings for the Arts
Contextual Architecture
Energy-Efficient Buildings
Engineering for Architecture
Great Houses for View Sites, Beach Sites, Sites in the Woods, Meadow Sites, Small Sites, Sloping Sites, Steep Sites and Flat Sites
Hospitals and Health Care Facilities, 2/e
Houses Architects Design for Themselves

Houses of the West
Institutional Buildings
Interior Spaces Designed by Architects
More Houses Architects Design for Themselves
Office Building Design, 2/e
Places for People: Hotels, Motels, Restaurants, Bars, Clubs, Community Recreation Facilities, Camps, Parks, Plazas and Playgrounds
Public, Municipal and Community Buildings
Religious Buildings
Recycling Buildings: Renovations, Remodelings, Restorations and Reuse
Techniques of Successful Practice
A Treasury of Contemporary Houses
25 Years of Record Houses

ARCHITECTURAL RECORD SERIES BOOKS

Ayers: Specifications for Architecture, Engineering and Construction
Feldman: Building Design for Maintainability
Heery: Time, Cost and Architecture

Heimsath: Behavioral Architecture
Hopf: Designer's Guide to OSHA
Portman and Barnett: The Architect As Developer

The articles in this book were written by the editors of Architectural Record. "Recycling Vancouver's Granville Island" was written by Michael and Julie Seelig.

Editors for the book were Patricia Markert and Joan Zseleczky. The designer was Laura Ierardi. Production supervisors were Carol Frances, assisted by Susan Stein, and Thomas G. Kowalczyk.

Printed and bound by Halliday Lithograph Corporation.

ISBN 0-07-002364-6

Library of Congress Cataloging in Publication Data
Main entry under title:

New life for old buildings.

"An Architectural record book."
Includes index.
1. Buildings—United States—Remodeling for other use. I. Schmertz, Mildred F.   II. Architectural record McGraw-Hill, Inc.
NA2793.N48   720'.28'6   81-11728
                                        AACR2

CONTENTS

PREFACE

The preservation and recycling of old buildings was once a cause celebre, ardently fought for by a small elite of architecture buffs ranked against a majority of believers in "progress" defined as the substitution of brand new buildings in modern style for decrepit old-fashioned ones.

Today in US cities and towns, preservation and recycling are commonplace. This change of attitude toward our heritage of buildings began in the 1960s when preservation first became a national issue. The movement gained impetus with the National Historic Preservation Act of 1966 and has been aided by the passage of subsequent legislation such as Section 2124 of the Tax Reform Act of 1976. This law encourages owners of historic property to use it for income or the conduct of business by allowing them to deduct or depreciate remodelling or restoration costs. It discourages such owners from destroying their historic structures by disallowing both the deduction of demolition expenses and the accelerated depreciation of the new structure built on the site. In addition, there are various local preservation laws. New York City's J-51 program, for example, offers a deduction and an exemption to developers who convert old, not necessarily historic buildings such as industrial lofts into housing.

Today, as a consequence, developers, once the arch foes of the friends of old buildings, have become preservationists themselves. They even call what they do "restoration"—to the dismay of specialists for whom genuine restoration is a demanding and scholarly pursuit only warranted by buildings of major historic or esthetic value.

The tax incentives which have elevated mere developers into "preservationists" and their work into "restoration" have come about because of new ways of looking at old buildings. The beginning of disillusionment with the industrial esthetic of Modern Architecture brought its corollary—a deepening regard for handmade ornamental buildings built of time-honored materials. People began to feel that the new architecture was inhuman and empty of meaning. Old architecture, on the other hand, seemed full of human reference.

Then there was the energy crisis. It became clear to many people that more energy was used to tear down and build anew than to fix. Furthermore, owners and their architects discovered what occupants of older buildings knew all along—such thick walled, cross-ventilated, attic covered old structures were often naturally cooler in summer and warmer in winter than new buildings.

Finally, inflation has increased all the costs of new construction, especially the cost of borrowing money. Since recycling uses less of everything, it is cheaper, and it appears to be here to stay.

This book includes examples of most kinds of recycling. Not all have been recycled solely to make or save money. Some buildings have been preserved, as they sustain old uses or launch new ones, principally because of the importance of the buildings themselves—be they fine works of architecture or important and widely loved civic or campus landmarks. A few of these, the Hall of Languages at Syracuse University, for example, have been completely rebuilt on the interior ("over recycled" in the opinion of some), while left intact on the exterior. Others like the Old Federal Courts Building in St. Paul have maintained the esthetic of "oldness" inside as well as out.

Among the projects included in this book which were designed for profit — the urban marketplaces, showrooms, and restaurants — the esthetic effort tends to be a juxtaposition of the new and slick against the old—separating and clarifying old and new so that each is distinct and enhanced by the contrast.

To recycle, of course, is not always the best thing to do to a fine old building. Many are ruined in the process, particularly since landmark laws do not protect their interiors. More architects and developers should begin to consider adapting a building's use in ways which would allow them to leave the building itself alone. Doing little or nothing at all to a building beyond necessary repairs to the roof and mechanical systems is another form of recycling. Physical alterations made by the user would be flexible and transitory in response to changing functions.

This last concept which urges that physical alterations be minimized wherever possible in favor of ordinary maintenance shows how far we have come from the era in which belief in "progress" made us tear down everything in sight. Today, recycling takes place between and includes the two opposite poles of scholarly restoration and common repairs. Altogether it has come to mean the conservation and renewal of our entire built world.

MILDRED F. SCHMERTZ

1

The preservation-conservation concept, as applied to the downtown commercial areas of our cities and towns, is not a simple one. The concept can mean the restoration of an historic building to its exact condition at some selected point in time, allowing it to function as it always has, or more likely it can mean that an historic building becomes a museum. Preservation-conservation can also mean the adaptation of a building's form and structure to serve either a modification or a complete change of use. Such efforts may be extended to include entire neighborhoods or districts, requiring the re-definition and enhancement of street patterns and public spaces as well as buildings.

The most convincing argument for conservation of neighborhoods or districts is that it revitalizes them economically, socially, and esthetically. And lately old buildings have begun to be seen as a source of energy conservation. For example, the US Department of Energy has estimated that it takes one gallon of gasoline to make, deliver, and install eight bricks for a new building. And some of the gasoline wasted by excessive automobile use can be saved by creating new shopping and recreational facilities in the declining commercial areas within short walking or public transportation distance from in-town residential neighborhoods.

The projects shown in this chapter are all essentially urban marketplaces. The first, Faneuil Hall Marketplace in Boston, consists of three adjacent early 19th-century market buildings in Greek Revival style. Rather than meticulously restoring these buildings, developer James W. Rouse and architects Benjamin Thompson Associates elected to adapt them in sophisticated ways to attract today's shoppers. This

URBAN
MARKETPLACES

modernization, however, has been sensitive and discreet; the buildings still appear genuinely old and can be enjoyed as such, especially in juxtaposition to the slick modern alterations which include glass-enclosed dining and shopping-terraces, bright canopies and modern graphics. Other urban marketplaces in this chapter which have been transformed for modern use rather than merely restored are the Old-town Mall in Baltimore and the Market House in Washington, DC.

Buildings which were not originally markets have also been included. The Cleveland Arcade in Cleveland, patterned after similar spaces in Europe, is now a modern shopping center; in Pittsburgh a former banking room, now the Bank Center, has a well-planned mix of uses; and the old Pennsylvania and Lake Erie railroad station is now a restaurant.

Entire neighborhoods and districts are being adapted for modern commercial use and this chapter includes one in Salem, Massachusetts. Finally, in Vancouver, British Columbia, the former manufacturing and warehouse buildings of Granville Island, once zoned for industry, have been transformed into a public market, shops, restaurants, and arts and crafts galleries. The island's old wharf spaces are being developed into badly needed in-town recreational space, allowing visitors to the island to combine shopping with leisure time activities.

All the cities with marketplaces included in this chapter — Boston, Baltimore, Washington, Cleveland, Pittsburgh, and Vancouver have suffered from declining downtowns. All of the recycled buildings shown are serving as important catalysts for revival.

1
BOSTON'S HISTORIC FANEUIL HALL MARKETPLACE: RESTORED AND TRANSFORMED BY ARCHITECT BENJAMIN THOMPSON AND DEVELOPER JAMES ROUSE

The photo above, taken from the window of the Mayor's office in City Hall is of Faneuil Hall Marketplace before the demolition of the roofs and certain facades of the North and South Market buildings began in December 1972. Faneuil Hall is in the foreground and directly behind is the Quincy Market building with its great dome and Classic Revival porches (right). The three rows of buildings were designed as an ensemble by Alexander Parris and built on landfill facing the harbor between 1824 and 1826.

Parris worked in granite, setting it upright on its small dimension, similar to wood post-and-beam construction, allowing window and door openings to be large for their time.

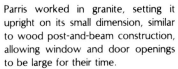

Long before he got the chance to restore the market, Benjamin Thompson had lovingly recorded the fine old buildings with his camera.

The great, elliptical, ribbed interior dome—long concealed by a hung ceiling—has been restored.

The two streets, closed to traffic, have become great public plazas, paved with brick, cobblestone and granite and newly planted with trees. Glass canopies extend the retail space into the plazas. In the market are meat, fish, cheese, produce and bakery goods as well as a variety of places to eat. The push carts are for small entrepreneurs who hope to graduate to shops.

In the South Market are to be found medium-priced to expensive women's and men's clothing, accessories, furniture, jewelry and gifts in 50 speciality shops. Office space is being leased on the third, fourth and loft levels of the buildings and four restaurants have been added. The drawing opposite shows the complete Marketplace.

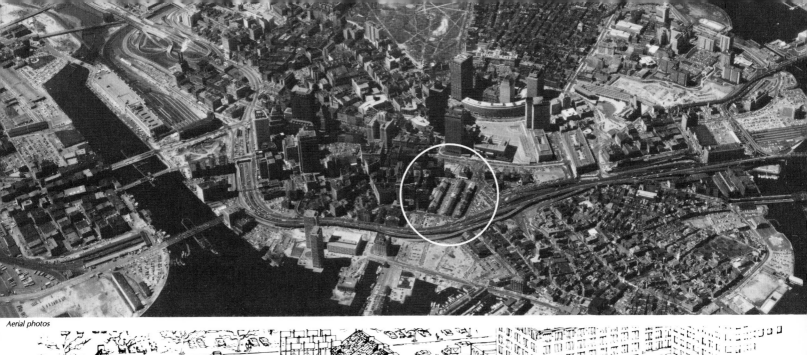

Photos courtesy Benjamin Thompson and Associates

The story of Faneuil Hall Marketplace goes back more than 150 years to 1823 and the decision by Mayor Josiah Quincy to build a new market hall adjacent to the original Faneuil Hall, which had been enlarged by Charles Bulfinch in 1805. In 1824, the splendid Greek Revival ensemble (opposite page top right), designed by Alexander Parris, was begun on new landfill facing the harbor. The north and south blocks were built by individual owners following Parris' design to harmonize with the city-constructed Quincy Market.

By 1959, after about 130 years of intensive use, the Marketplace was in danger of being declared obsolete and torn down. Steps were being taken to build a larger wholesale center away from the city to which the merchants were expected to move. In 1966, architect Frederick A. Stahl, a trustee of the Society for the Preservation of New England Antiquities, and Roger Webb, head of Architectural Heritage, Inc. (both non-profit organizations), went to the Boston Redevelopment Authority proposing that they do a complete preservation-modernization study for the Marketplace. Their comprehensive report, commissioned in 1968 by Edward J. Logue, head of the BRA, led to a HUD grant to Boston of $2 million, to underwrite the cost of building restoration.

Stahl's architectural firm, Stahl/Bennett, Inc., was then hired by the BRA to begin the exterior restoration and renovation of the market buildings, creating the framework for construction to be done by the yet-to-be-selected developer.

In October 1970, the BRA published its developers' kit for bids on the three market blocks: 6.5 acres of prime urban land and 370,000 square feet of space. In June 1971 the BRA named the winning proposal and development team: Benjamin Thompson & Associates (architect) and Van Arkle-Moss (developer). In January 1972 this team was "de-designated" for failure to get funding. In April of that year the BRA invited bids for the exterior renovation of the North-South Market Streets, using the $2 million HUD grant and the Stahl/Bennett drawings and specifications, and in June selected a contractor. In May 1972 James W. Rouse, head of the Rouse Company, notified the BRA of his desire to become the developer with Benjamin Thompson as his architect. What happened after that is described on pages 12–13.

Thompson makes photographs of good signs from all over the world (above), which he uses to persuade Rouse Company tenants to improve their graphics. He also favors straightforward methods of display as in the Market's old days (below).

The 1968 feasibility study, by Architectural Heritage, Inc, and the Society for the Preservation of New England Antiquities, was carried out by Frederick A. Stahl, Roger Webb, William Endicott, vice president of the SPNEA and Walter Muir Whitehill, who was then director and librarian of the Boston Athenaeum and a member of the Massachusetts Historical Commission. They produced a five-volume report including an historical study, a combined urban design, architectural and engineering report, a volume of technical drawings, another devoted to specifications and cost estimates and a final volume devoted to real estate, marketing, development and disposition proposals. Of great interest is their documentation of the historic importance of the buildings. Their report shows that within the limitations of the Greek Revival style, new technological innovations were employed, such as the use of cast-iron columns, iron tension rods, laminated wood ribs for the copper-covered dome and the first large-scale use of granite and glass in an unusual post-and-beam technique. As time passed (top and middle) the buildings declined (bottom).

In their words: "Our goal is *genuineness*. This is a better word than authenticity, which is too often used to mean a good imitation of something genuine. Genuineness is the real thing. It is the real cobblestone street on which earlier generations walked and worked. It is solid wood, not plastic veneer, old wood genuinely aged, not new wood stained. It is stone that shows the marks of time, treads worn by generations of feet. It has meaning because it puts us in the presence of what was—the experience of history—not a later impression of what something 'looked like.' Without a clear relation to what is genuine, our sense of values and ability to judge real from fake is damaged—or worse, never developed.

"Two rules of restoration seem well accepted now after some recent years of confusion: First, do not improve on history; do not 'restore back' to a fixed cut-off date; history is richer in time than any one period or style. Second, when repair or replacement of building elements is required, new material should be subtly distinguished from the original. If such distinctions are not made, the genuineness of the original is confused, and the viewers' perception of time is confused. A third precept is longer in coming, but achieves more acceptance daily. This is the principle of *valid continuity*—the joining of successive styles in elegant and compatible ways. If the joining of what is old and what is contemporary (in whatever year) is clearly differentiated, the genuineness of each can be established and enhanced. Throughout Europe and America, buildings of successive periods have used differing materials, proportions and details. Cumulatively, these changes express the depth of a time line in the life of a building, which is one of architecture's most important perspectives on history. Buildings like people must be allowed to age, develop and change—and the changes must show. Buildings, like people, cannot be asked to stand still at a perfect 21, like a blushing beauty embalmed in a wax museum, or an aging movie star restored to youth by plastic surgery. We should not attempt to freeze history but rather strive to enhance its flow. The market should be neither 'historic' or 'modern' but simply the genuine continuation of a special place in city life growing tastefully out of genuine urban commerce and answering human needs."

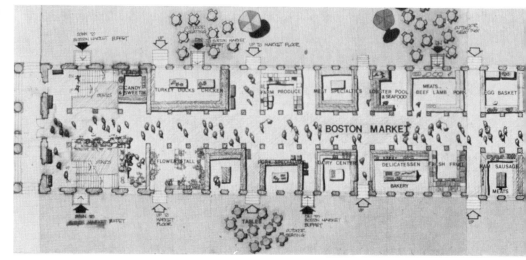

The models and drawings produced by the office of Benjamin Thompson and Associates have a freshness and appearance of spontaneity which belies the dead earnestness behind them. The sketch above is part of a retail feasibility study for the Quincy Market building. Ben Thompson has been called a "real merchant" by Rouse, who should know. The feasibility study shows the kinds of foods to be sold in the market, in what sequence and the number of square feet and linear feet of counter each tenant might require. The plan indicates seating areas where the shopper can rest and eat the snacks he has bought off the stands. The drawing below is one of many made for the Thompsons by Judy Maiewski to help convince non-believers that the Marketplace could be the lively place it has become.

Benjamin Thompson (left) and James Rouse (middle) show their models and drawings to Mayor Kevin H. White (right). The occasion was the designation by the BRA, under the recommendation of its then director Robert Kenny, of the Rouse Company as developer.

Photos courtesy Benjamin Thompson and Associates

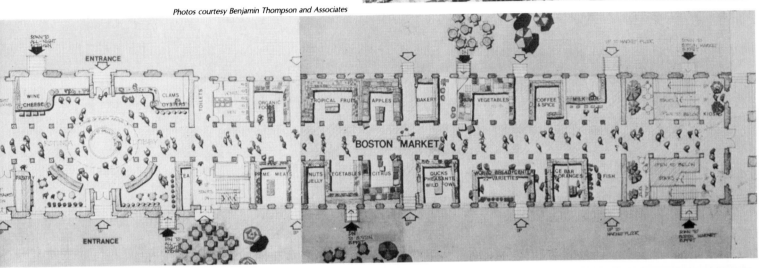

Benjamin Thompson was first associated with the developer Van Arkle-Moss, who had been designated by the BRA to lease and transform the Faneuil Hall Marketplace into a viable commercial center. When this developer failed to get financing, their designation was rescinded. Architect Thompson, however, was determined not to lose the opportunity to help direct the development of the Marketplace according to design and merchandising principles which he believed would assure the success of the project. From January to April of 1972, he tried to induce one developer after another to associate with him, only to have the project rejected as unfeasible. Finally, at the suggestion of Robert Simon, the developer of the new town of Reston, he wrote a letter to James W. Rouse, the developer of the new town of Columbia. Rouse is chairman of the board of the Rouse Company, one of the nation's leading real estate development and mortgage banking firms. He has built 26 retail centers in the United States and Canada as he continues to develop Columbia for an eventual population of 100,000.

Rouse wanted to try his hand at a downtown development in the belief that the future holds great opportunities in the downtown centers of cities. Thompson and his wife and business partner Jane in her words: "presented him with the whole Faneuil Hall Marketplace package. We had the figures, the feasibility, the whole thing was ready-made. It came together in his head and he was ready to try it." Until the Thompsons' entrepreneurial effort to interest Rouse in the Marketplace, however, nothing had come along that could work.

"All the sites I had been offered," says Rouse, "were tiny little islands in the midst of jungles—their environments weren't big enough, reassuring enough." Rouse found the atmosphere surrounding the Boston site to be very encouraging. He was able to see that, in his words: "Boston is a city that is still strong in its heart. I was impressed with the development of the waterfront, the proposed new $3.5 million park, the Mercantile Building, the financial district and the nearness of City Hall." Things had indeed come together at the right time to attract a developer of Rouse's intelligence to downtown Boston.

The Marketplace is located between two of the BRA's most ambitious undertakings of the past twenty years: the $230 million Government Center and the $125 million Waterfront Redevelopment Project. Within the last ten years, public investment in the waterfront project has been more than $40 million. All of this effort was beginning to show when Rouse made his first visit to the old Marketplace. Venerable wharf buildings on three of Boston's great old piers had been or were being rehabilitated into housing, shops and restaurants. The new Aquarium had recently been completed. The waterfront's Atlantic Avenue was being redone. Rouse observed as well that the Faneuil Hall neighborhood could become the vital heart of the larger improved area. This extends beyond the waterfront northwestward to Government Center—which in addition to City Hall and its great plaza is crammed with other high-density city, state and Federal office buildings—and southwestward to a cluster of high-rise privately constructed new office buildings, proposed, underway or completed. In his mind's eye, Rouse could see thousands of office workers on their lunch hour eating and shopping in the Marketplace, picking up goodies on their way home, and returning to the restaurants and theaters at night. Just as important to Rouse were the 20,000 people who live within walking distance of the Marketplace. In addition to the new housing that was being created, the old North End residential neighborhood was still alive and the whole area was becoming busy and prosperous enough to give a sense of security, even at night. But downtown needed a revitalized core to be as Jane Thompson puts it: "the final burst of energy to make everything really wake up."

Rouse also noted on this momentous first visit that the entire improved area is accessible by well located subway stops at Government Center and at the Aquarium, and that it is possible, furthermore, to take a subway from Logan Airport directly to these stops. Downtown Boston, moreover, is one of the best cities in the world to walk in. The Quincy Market streets were to become part of a pedestrian network that includes a lovely walk from Charles Bulfinch's golden-domed State House at the crown of Beacon Hill, past Boston Common, through the magnificent spaces within and surrounding City Hall, downward to Faneuil Market and on to the harbor with its 4.5-acre Waterfront Park. Rouse owes his success to never forgetting that shopping and eating should be a pleasure as well as a necessity, and he could see that the Marketplace would be just the place for people out walking for fun to relax, eat, browse and buy. And for those arriving by car the Market is adjacent to thruway exits, a large parking garage at Government Center, and other convenient parking facilities.

As important as the strength and vitality of the Marketplace's surroundings were the old buildings themselves. "They didn't require a lot of twisting, turning and remaking," says Rouse. "I could see that handling them just as they were we could produce a logical, workable marketplace." Rouse, however, did not and does not venerate the buildings as the architectural historians do. "I don't think we saved something beautiful because I don't think the Market was beautiful, not even long ago. I think that together with Ben Thompson we have created something beautiful out of the opportunity that was there. This is a lot more than restoration. Of course what we have done would not have the feeling that it does if the buildings hadn't been old and rather marvelous to begin with. Those big granite openings and that wonderful rotunda and dome!"

Convinced by his first visit to the Market, by the Thompsons' arguments and supported by subsequent feasibility studies made by his staff, Rouse with the Thompsons began the effort to persuade the City of Boston and the BRA to designate the Rouse Company as developer and to arrange the financing—two interrelated and highly complex tasks. Thompson, now Rouse's architect, set about to help his new client by sharing the results of at least twenty years of thinking about ways to revitalize the downtowns of cities. He also had to offer his particular type of urban retailing experience—bringing together all kinds of goods in a marketplace setting—learned through founding and (for some years) owning and managing Design Research.

"Ben is a merchant," says Rouse. "He understands with us the things that are essential to a marketplace—how to stimulate certain kinds of traffic so that one type of purchase leads to another. Shops must be easy to find and enjoyable to be in. Shopping can be entertaining. Ben understands this." And Thompson offered Rouse firm counsel on just how far to

The Marketplace, although a great success, is not usually *this* crowded. The occasion: August 26, 1976, the 150th anniversary of the Market and its rededication and opening in honor of the Bicentennial. Mayor White, James Rouse, the Thompsons and BRA director Robert Kenny were there along with thousands of Bostonians eager to discover their reborn downtown.

acknowledge standards of historical exactitude in the restoration of buildings, which are at the same time being adapted to today's marketing requirements. Thompson, for example, substituted large single panes of glass for the old ten-over-ten multi-paned windows of the early nineteenth century—against the opposition of preservationists advising the BRA.

It took six months of intensive effort for Rouse and the Thompsons to get the City of Boston to designate the Rouse Company as developer. Finally, in May 1974, the lease was signed and in July of that year Rouse got a commitment of $21 million from Teachers Insurance and Annuity for the permanent financing. Two weeks later Rouse got a commitment from Chase Manhattan for $10.5 million—one-half of the construction financing, on the condition that he get the remainder from Boston banks. Another six months went by until ten Boston financial institutions finally came up with the other half and only then after Rouse had broken the project up into three phases, the first, Quincy Market, to cost $7.5 million. The GBH Macomber Company finally began construction of Phase One in 1975.

The reluctance of the financial community to lend money to the Rouse Company indicates that at that time the banks saw substantial risks in the project. There was fear and uncertainty about the concept of retailing in an urban area, based upon the record of failures in the downtowns of many U.S. cities. Further, the costs of remodeling old buildings is difficult to estimate accurately because of unforeseen problems leading to a fear that construction costs would get out of hand. Adding to the uncertainty was the fact that Rouse was embarking upon an unconventional retailing scheme in which there was to be no major retail tenant.

Their idea was that each tenant should lease a small selling area designed to maximize his sales per square foot allowing him to pay a higher rent per square foot. There would be more tenants per square foot than in a major shopping center and the likelihood of more turnover. Such tenants were expected by the banks to have lower credit ratings than typical major tenants.

In a typical shopping center there are two major tenants. For example, in the Chestnut Hill shopping center, the latest to be constructed in the Boston area, there are branches of Bloom-

ingdale's and Filene's. The bankers took a risk on financing the rest of the space to be constructed because the draw of magnets like Bloomingdale's and Filene's would bring customers and additional tenants to the center.

At Faneuil Hall Market, however, there was no certainty as to who the tenants would be and therefore what the attraction would be. The bankers knew, because Thompson and Rouse had told them in every way they knew how, that the way the tenants were located in the space in its entirety would be the magnet— and this is how it has turned out. But it took imagination, and lenders are not celebrated for risking that kind of imagination. Finally, in order to get his loan, Rouse did have to agree to lease 10,000 square feet on the second floor of Quincy Market to the Magic Pan, the only large tenant in the Marketplace.

At the point at which Boston's lenders began to relent, the city, state and Federal investment was close to $10 million. The project cost to the Rouse Company was to be $30 million; which included in addition to construction costs, design, legal work and the costs of getting the tenants in place. Thus the public subsidy was approximately one-third. The usual ratio is about ten per cent.

The cost of rehabilitating the space came to between $65 to $75 per rentable square foot. Some of the retail space cost as much as $100 per square foot to renovate. Without this level of public subsidy, the rents would have been out of sight. No developer could have done the job.

According to Jane Thompson, the cost to Rouse of the reconstruction of the market buildings and getting the space ready for the tenants was about 10 per cent higher than in a large shopping center. The shopping center developer is used to building shells. Rebuilding the Faneuil Hall Marketplace was more expensive and complicated, but the Rouse Company, which charges its tenants a rent based upon a certain percentage of their sales, is getting its investment back at the rate of 200 per cent of what they normally get for retail space in a typical suburban shopping center. The Market is such a success that some shops are doing business at the rate of $400 of sales per square foot per month. Rouse believes his gamble was well worth it.

According to Stuart Forbes, who has been

the Boston Redevelopment Authority's representative in working out the financial feasibility of the project with Roy Williams, the Rouse Company's director of the Marketplace operation, Rouse's most important strength was his ability to put together enough tenants of the right type so that when the Marketplace opened, its character was immediately evident. After filling the Quincy Market building with various kinds of merchants of food and drawing great crowds thereby, it was then easier to attract the fashionable clothing, accessory, jewelry and gift shops which have opened a year later in the South Market.

Rouse is particularly proud of his pushcarts: "We wanted to create as many independent tenants as we could so we decided to give small merchants a chance with pushcarts. We hired a bright young woman who went out all over New England identifying artists and craftsmen and small entrepreneurs with narrow specialties. She worked on 900 prospects for those 43 pushcarts, evaluating and recruiting them. We designed the carts and provided boxes and baskets to hang on them. Our standard lease with a tenant is 44 pages long and requires the merchant to have a lawyer, accountant, contractor and architect. So we created a one-page lease so that somebody could bring in his silk-screened whatevers and in a week or so he could tell if they would sell." Rouse believes that the carts have been a great drawing card for the Marketplace. At least one pushcart operator has graduated to a small shop in the South Market.

The Rouse Company now pays taxes that are between 20 and 25 per cent of the gross income generated—which is consistent with other tax agreements in Boston. There was tax abatement during construction in return for contributions the Rouse Company made to the city, notably the installation and funding of Boston's Bicentennial exhibit in the Quincy Building. Rouse also assumed the risks inherent in the structural repairs contract, and did some other construction work which was previously to have been done by the city. The land and buildings are owned by the City of Boston and the Rouse Company has a 99-year lease. According to Stuart Forbes, the Faneuil Hall Marketplace will, within five years, be generating in excess of $1 million in real estate taxes per year.

2
RECYCLING OLD BUILDINGS INTO DOWNTOWN MARKETPLACES

Urban marketplaces are as old as towns themselves. Those being planned and built today, however, give form to new merchandising ideas. They generate new and profitable ways to sell goods and bring life as well as money back into cities. They still need the excitement that comes from a mix of social, cultural and entertainment activities—as well as commerce—all happening in one place at the same time; here, one meets friends, has new experiences, sees and is seen while conducting one's business. But today, the urban marketplace reflects greatly altered economic and social climates. Basic necessities can be bought elsewhere. The new downtown market has to offer something special.

As an assemblage of diverse small entrepreneurs, marketplaces seem to buck recent planning thought that has separated retail, entertainment and cultural functions in different locations. They also challenge typical chain store and bulk sales operations. But while consumers may be falling into increasing conformity in their buying habits, they appear to want more diversity of choice. Cash register receipts attest to this at San Francisco's Ghirardelli Square and Seattle's Pioneer Square. So does International Shopping Center Council president James Wilson Jr.: "The smaller centers with smaller stores serving more clearly defined trade areas are going to be the order. There will be a decided move back to urban areas. And rehabilitation, conversion and expansion is already the dominant character of shopping center investment." Of course, true marketplaces are more than shopping centers, but the message is clear.

The successful urban marketplace is as much spirit as it is planning. In fact, to be really successful, it will hardly *seem* to be planned at all. According to Wendy Tsuji at ELS Design Group: "Mixed uses have always been with us, until modern planners planned them away." But even the term "mixed use" may seem too much like planning to catch the spirit. Jane Jacobs would have put it more bluntly, when she said that people must have old-fashioned streets and cities to survive. "Damn the planners." Nonetheless, planning is vital. And this is what separates modern markets from historic ones. Underneath the exuberance, rational control has to be firmly at work. Lack of planning produced such spontaneous successes as St. Louis's Gaslight Square, and as quickly destroyed them. Accordingly, the following pages will thoroughly explore the new, more responsive kind of planning behind many examples of the new kind of marketplace.

Otto Baitz

Clemens Kalischer

A marketplace can be a building like the Victorian structure recently renovated in Salem, Massachusetts (below), or the Bank Center in Pittsburgh (above). In the Center, architects IKM Partnership and Lorenzi Dodds & Gunnill have used 100,000 square feet on three levels in the original banking room and surrounding spaces for a well planned mix of uses. True marketplaces have many activities which are highly visible at once, such as open stalls exposed to view. A lively center of attraction can also be created within a dramatic space such as the Cleveland Arcade (right). According to architect Herbert McLaughlin, reviving the ailing fortunes of a mixed retail and commercial building like this can often mean little more than new approaches to merchandising. The original building was completed in 1980 by architects John Eisenman and George Horatio Smith.

John Landsberg

Clemens Kalischer

There are three basic forms that marketplaces can take—sheds, arcades and streets. Washington's Market House (pages 20-21) is a classic example of the shed. But the really ambitious nineteenth century city looked to the dramatic galleries and arcades of contemporary Europe for inspiration. The Cleveland Arcade in Cleveland, Ohio (see photo previous page) is the largest such arcade in the United States. Architects Kaplan/McLaughlin/Diaz are in the process of restoring it to its former grandeur. Herbert McLaughlin has a dual role as architect and partner in developers Cohnner & McLaughlin. He says that the Arcade is really more of an ancestor of the shopping mall than a market, because its commercial activities were discreetly concealed behind storefronts that ringed the multi-story central space. Still, the drama of this space and the social activities that occur in it give the building a focus that must have been even more pronounced when it was "the only show in town." McLaughlin's work is both physical and financial. By a basic renovation, steadily upgrading graphics and seeking more profitable tenants (the developers started three stores on their own), they have managed to bring the once-deteriorating building back into solvency again, although they are far from finished. Indeed, architects all over the country are becoming involved in a direct financial way in re-cycling older buildings. One, William Downing, bought the massive surplus high school in Ithaca, New York and has converted it into apartments, offices and a shopping concourse, which has contributed to the downtown area's revival.

Another building that has been converted to a market, the Bank Center in Pittsburgh (see photo on page 14) also has a dramatic space that was a former banking room. Architects IKM Partnership and Lorenzi Dodds & Gunnill have used three levels in this room and surrounding spaces to full advantage for a well planned mix of uses. Here, forty per cent of the floor area is devoted to food and entertainment, ten per cent to two movie theaters and the remainder to open retail stalls. According to architect Jim Morgan, who is executive vice president of the client firm, Pittsburgh Real Estate Services Corporation, the initial popularity of the market part of the Center carried adjacent renovated offices through a weak market period, and stimulated their eventual success.

Another way to create a marketplace is to design a street to be one. One of the first to be completed as part of a community renewal project is Oldtown Mall in Baltimore by Architects O'Malley & Associates (right bottom). It is different from the usual market, because it is located in a disadvantaged neighborhood instead of a central business district, and it fulfills more traditional roles of providing basic necessities. It is the extension of two long existing market sheds to benefit neighboring retail establishments. Several blocks of an intersecting street were closed to all but pedestrian traffic, and an intensive program of improvement was aimed at facade renovation, graphics, lighting and street furniture. The renovation spurred sizable private as well as public investment.

At Oldtown Mall in Baltimore, (photos left) architects O'Malley & Associates have extended two existing market buildings by closing an intersecting street. The Prospect of Westport restaurant in Kansas City (right) has been remodeled by the Architects Copartnership/McCoyHutchinson Stone as part of the Westport Square Shopping District in a newly revitalized historic district. Salem, Massachusetts (RECORD, December 1977) may become one of the first cities in the U.S. to complete its downtown redevelopment plan. The sensitive mix of new and restored commercial residential and retail buildings (above) has just won an environmental award from HUD.

Dan Whitney

Clemens Kalischer

Perhaps the most important contribution that the marketplace concept can make to a city's economy is the revival of underloved or derelict areas. The President's Advisory Council on Historic Preservation recently completed an exhaustive study of four restoration-oriented efforts to show just how large these contributions might be. In Galveston's Strand, retail sales rose 125 per cent over a four-year pre-inflationary period. Property values and tax revenues rose almost 50 per cent in Alexandria, Virginia. And the nine square blocks of Seattle's Pioneer Square—once a derelict and run-down area—have been turned into a safe and prosperous marketplace. Savannah, the fourth city studied by the President's Advisory Council, has already spent massive amounts of money on its historic downtown business district, with highly successful results. Now, Savannah has a new plan by the Parsons Brinkerhoff Development Corporation to turn its extensive unused railroad yards on a nearby 40-acre site into a new $70-million urban center with an emphasis on tourism. Called Battle Park, it is to have hotel, residential, office, convention and performing-arts facilities. These are to be given focal liveliness by a retail-entertainment marketplace located in some of the currently most dilapidated maintenance buildings, which include a romantic roundhouse (see photo and rendering right). Almost all of the site's impressive array of early nineteenth-century industrial architecture will be retained. Included are a handsome group of period administration buildings facing the downtown area at the site's edge, which are to be renovated for their original use as offices. Also along this edge is the original terminal building, which has already been recycled into Savannah's visitors' center.

Architects Perry Lord, the president and Richard Heidelberger, the project director for the Development Corporation are pursuing such building reclamation projects all across the country. According to Heidelberger: "The complications in the process are enormous, but the rewards can be as well." On the Savannah proposal, he went through six months of public hearings on alternate plans to get the many public groups to give approval to the final scheme. With both development and design arms in a single organization, and considerable financial backing, the Corporation promises great things for both conservation and profit efforts. Other projects currently in the works include the conversion of Bridgeport, Connecticut's 1929 Hotel Barnum into housing for the elderly, retail and commercial space, and a similar conversion of a factory building in Ozone Park in New York City. Another project in Massachusetts is described in the caption. The first such reclamation project that the firm has completed is a restaurant and office complex in a former industrial building built in the 1880s in Concord, New Hampshire, where the firms is active in other downtown revival projects.

Unused railroad yards and structures can make marketplaces. The buildings are available, often sturdy, and can have large dramatic spaces—such as the former concourse of Pittsburgh's P&LE railroad station (above), now a restaurant by architects Roger Sherman Associates. Plans for Nashville's Union Station (right) call for an extensive mixed-used development. Savannah's railroad yards (left) are to be turned into another mixed-use development by the Parson's Brinckerhoff Development Corporation (rendering right). Another project being planned by PBDC is the recycling of a mill in Chicopee, Massachusetts (below) into housing and shops.

Mark Johnson

3
CONTEMPORARY MERCHANDISING PRINCIPLES REVIVE AN HISTORIC BUILDING TYPE: MARKET HOUSE IN WASHINGTON, D.C.

Built as a market in 1865 for what was then the separate suburb of Georgetown, this small building is a classic survivor of the covered centralized marketplace boasted by most small towns in the United States at that time. Despite its relatively modest size—40 by 200 feet—it was long the local hub of commercial and social activity. Because farmers stopped coming there to set up their stalls around 1935, its existence was threatened. It was protected, however, by covenants on site usage in the original deed, and it stumbled further into the twentieth century as the Square Deal Supermarket and then as a wholesale auto-parts distributorship.

In their plan to revitalize Markethouse on more traditional lines, architects Clark Tribble Harris & Li have employed current retailing techniques that once more make a social setting work. According to partner Jerry Li: "You have to give the clientele what it can't get in supermarkets—whether it's a special ambiance or unusual merchandise." The architects have opted for a lot of both. There are careful controls of lighting and tenant graphics and a tight circulation system that is uniquely desirable in this type of retailing. Awnings both inside and outside of windows help to control natural light in order to heighten the theatrical effect and to present a consistent design.

At the official opening recently, nineteen diverse food operations occupied spaces ranging in size from 72 to 530 square feet. These included butchers and green-grocers, purveyors of condiments and ready-made hors d'oeuvres to full meals, and a restaurant on the mezzanine to overlook the whole busy scene. The colorful result has a rich vibrant character and a liveliness that make it a place where people want to be.

THE MARKET HOUSE, Washington, D.C. Owner: *joint venture of the Western Development Corporation and the Donohoe Companies.* Architects: *Clark Tribble Harris & Li.* Engineers: *Tadjer-Cohen* (structural); *Gormley-Wareham Associates* (mechanical/electrical) *Vinsant Associates* (tenant mechanical/electrical). Consultants: *Peter Barna/Lighting Design* (lighting); *Design/Joe Sonderman Inc.* (graphics). General contractor: *Western Construction Company.*

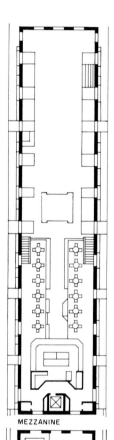

MEZZANINE

Despite the seeming casualness here, there is a design formula that similar plans would do well to heed. Architect Li likens the result to a stage set. Instead of supermarket-sized corridors, there are narrow ones that invite people to see the merchandise and each other at close range. Instead of bright even lighting, there are directed pinpoints that highlight the special nature of what is being sold. Instead of rows of standardized displays, there is a variety of stands with individual graphics, both encouraged and controlled by the architects to add to the bazaar-like flavor.

MAIN FLOOR

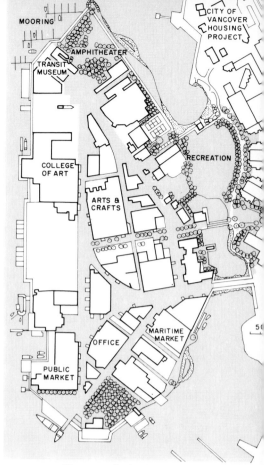

4
RECYCLING VANCOUVER'S GRANVILLE ISLAND

by Michael and Julie Seelig

"You should see the people we have down here! There are women in mink coats buying a few shallots while chauffeur-driven limousines wait outside. There are families shopping carefully for produce which is below supermarket prices. There are kids buying freshly baked cookies and doughnuts." The manager of the Granville Island Public Market sounded incredulous during his interview on a local radio station. The large crowds at the market and the mixture of people, from sleek sophisticates buying handmade pasta, to teenagers with backpacks snacking on roasted nuts, to the down and out, startled even the planners and managers of the island.

As one Vancouver developer commented, "You can do all the market research you want, but the big test is the opening week. If something is going to be a success, it will show then. If it doesn't go immediately, no amount of prodding and patching and gimmickry will help." The point of view may not always be true—many projects which are ultimately successful do get off to a slow start. But it certainly has proven true for Vancouver's Granville Island Public Market. From the day its doors opened, it has been a crowded, bustling success.

A magnificent setting

Granville Island, with its Public Market, theaters, restaurants, art school and factories, is a recycled industrial area along Vancouver's waterfront. It is another sign of the development boom this young city has been experiencing over the last decade. Vancouver is less than 100 years old, and during its recent surge in development, it seemed about to follow the pattern of other North American cities. High-rise offices were developed downtown, dominated by the office towers of Canada's major banks, towers which are strikingly similar in Toronto, Montreal and Vancouver. Yet Vancouver, because of its youth, has very few of the older landmarks which serve to soften the brashness of the new construction.

What the city does have, however, is a magnificent setting. From the foot of each of the major downtown streets there is a panoramic view across Burrard Inlet to the mountains, which appear to rise directly out of the sea. Vancouverites' attachment to these views became quite apparent in the early '70s

when citizen opposition prevented construction of both an office tower which would have obstructed the view from one of the downtown streets and of a high-rise tinted glass tower which the public feared would darken the city's skyline. In 1972 and 1973, these bouts of citizen opposition, such as the anti-"black tower" campaign and others, coalesced into a positive force in the city. The boosterism of the Chamber of Commerce and other civic organizations began to give way to a public awareness of the opportunities to make the city a unique environment whose man-made structures would be compatible with and worthy of the beautiful sea and mountains which surround them.

This change in attitude manifested itself politically in the election to City Council of a group of enlightened civic leaders who responded to public demands for more careful guidance of the city's development. A number of projects were undertaken which capitalized on Vancouver's assets and which responded to the local situation by developing appropriate "home-grown" solutions rather than by importing programs from other cities. Programs included rehabilitation of Gastown, Vancouver's original townsite, the down-zoning of the city's densest residential area, creation of a pedestrian mall on the main downtown street, rehabilitation of the Chinatown area, and development of the False Creek flats into one of the largest and most experimental in-town housing projects in North America.

Granville Island

Contiguous with the False Creek area, the "island" was actually once a sandbar in what is now called False Creek. In 1913 a bulkhead was built, and silt dredged from False Creek was pumped onto the site to form a new industrial area. The island is in fact a peninsula extending into False Creek Basin, an inlet formerly used for industrial purposes and now being redeveloped for housing, offices, marinas and public uses. Rising above the island is Granville Bridge, which adds to the industrial, "tough" character of the island. The bridge ramp, once considered a hopeless eyesore, is perceived today as adding a rough charm to the area.

When planning for redevelopment of Granville Island began in 1973, the island contained a number of functioning industrial operations, including a cement mixing plant and a steel factory. It also contained a number of vacant usable structures and some dilapidated ones. The jumble of industrial buildings represented both a challenge and an opportunity. The difficulties were obvious:

The over-all plan for the Island (above) indicates the general use areas, which include extensive markets and arts and crafts facilities. More generous recreational space was created by extending and improving wharf areas (below). The main street (opposite page) was photographed from the Granville Bridge.

Michael Seelig photos

Julie Seelig is a professional planner in private practice in Vancouver. Michael Y. Seelig is an architect, planner and Associate Professor of Planning in the School of Community and Regional Planning of the University of British Columbia in Vancouver. He is also a partner in the firm of Gutheim Seelig Erickson.

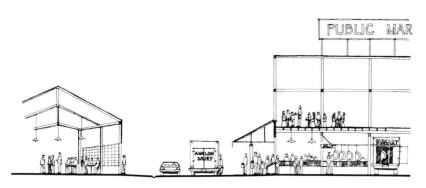

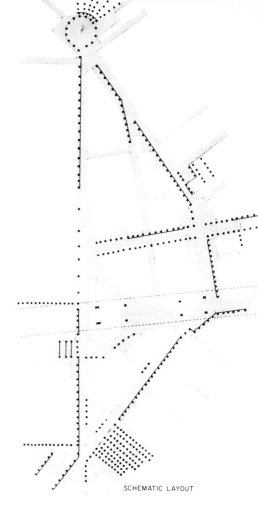

the street system was convoluted and whatever was not a building was a road; some existing industries, particularly the cement plant, were too large and costly to relocate; the Granville Bridge ramp rises directly above the 38-acre site; few residents had even heard of this ramshackle industrial area.

But two factors made the redevelopment of the island an almost romantic opportunity. First, the location—adjacent to downtown—is superb. The bridge ramp above the island is in fact the main access route to the center of the city. The "island" is surrounded on three sides by water, and the view of the boats moored nearby is charming. The adjacent False Creek housing development houses roughly 5,000 people who provide a ready market for the wide variety of services developed on the island.

Second, Granville Island belongs to a single owner, the federal government. In 1975, Vancouver's Member of Parliament, the Hon. Ron Basford, then Canada's Revenue Minister, arranged for a study of Granville Island to be commissioned through Canada Mortgage and Housing Corporation. The study, prepared by the Vancouver firm of Thompson, Berwick, Pratt and Partners, provided the initial framework of objectives to be realized, concept plans, development strategy and the administrative structure necessary for this undertaking. As a result of this report, the federal government made a major commitment to invest $25 million in the redevelopment project. Approximately $11 million went to buy out the remaining leases on industrial properties which were to be redeveloped for other uses. Single ownership of such a sizable parcel of land so close to downtown represented a unique opportunity for coordinating development within a single environmental theme.

Revival of a lost urbanity

In accordance with the recommendations of the report, a five-member board of trustees—the Granville Island Trust—was appointed to oversee the development of the island. At the outset, the Trust made the unusual decision to retain a large portion of the island's industry, including the massive Canada Cement factory. The new plan was to be woven around these existing uses and around the existing street pattern. The overall aim was to create a public recreation place both for residents of the newly developing False Creek area and for the community at large. Prior to the selection of Norman Hotson Architects, the urban designers for the project, the Trust itself established the over-

all concept plan and provided the urban designers with three strong directives: First, to assist the Canada Mortgage and Housing Corporation (the arm of the government administering the project) and an urban economic consultant in arriving at an appropriate development program and implementation strategies to create a public place; second, to design the public infrastructure for the island, including a network of streets and other open spaces, and to recycle certain buildings as key public projects; and third, to establish specific architectural guidelines for other building projects as they develop.

The urban designers found that the key task was to define what constitutes a contemporary public place, particularly in light of the industrial activities which were to continue on the island. Three concepts emerged in the definition of Granville Island as a place for public recreation—first, the revitalization plan aimed at "the revival of a lost urbanity." Through the juxtaposition of a wide variety of small-scale activities, the designers hoped to achieve a truly urban recreation spot. Now that several of the key developments are in place, particularly the Public Market and two theaters, it is plain to see that this plan has succeeded.

"Variety" and "diversity" are the key words in describing not only the people wandering through the Public Market and surrounding streets and shops, but also the nature of the entire Granville Island development. The broad goal for Granville Island is the regeneration of a level of urbanity generally lacking in our society today. The urban designers note that "randomness, curiosity, delight and surprise have all but disappeared [from our cities]. There is a growing concern amongst our citizens that real urbanity not be lost everywhere, and it is intended that it be encouraged to flourish on Granville Island." The island represents a return to that period before zoning sterilized our urban environments—the period when a single city street contained bars, furniture workshops, a tailor, and a corner grocery store. A second factor in making the island a public place was the designers' concept of an "opportunity place," a place for those uses which are interesting but have difficulty finding space to lease elsewhere in the city. So the island redevelopment has provided space for artists' studios, theaters, workshops, and, of course, the public produce market. The third concept involved in creating a public place was the idea of promoting active rather than passive recreation. The Trust was careful to focus on activities which are very public in

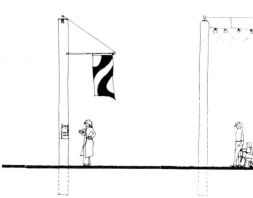

SCHEMATIC LAYOUT

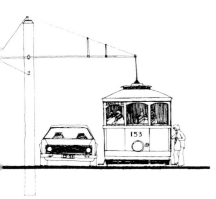

The drawings on this and the opposite page show the poles, pipes, canopies, lighting and pavings which are the basic design elements that unify the Island, and the photos indicate specific uses. The interior of the Public Market (left) shows the use of this system to carry indoor lighting fixtures. The new Arts Club Theater (above) is located on the market plaza.

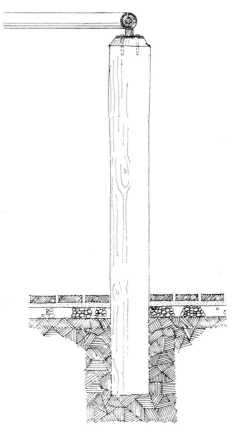

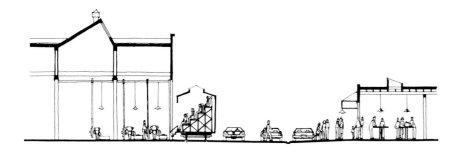

nature, such as the market; activities in which people become involved, as in arts and crafts studios; and activities where people see and learn about something new, as in the production of hand-forged chain and other industrial processes.

A unique job of recycling

The location and the single ownership of Granville Island have provided unique opportunities to develop an unusual and even romantic public place. The original feel of the area has been kept throughout the redevelopment. The island was an industrial section that grew into a jumble of streets and buildings with cranes, winches, and trucks throughout. The approach has not been to prettify and sanitize the place, à la Ghirardelli Square in San Francisco or Pioneer Square in Seattle. The project sets a precedent in recycling a whole area while retaining existing industries. It creates a mixture of cultural, educational, commercial, and industrial uses as opposed to the more typical recycling of industrial buildings for commercial and office purposes only.

Tenant selection has been based on the following checklist developed by Norman Hotson, Architects: 1. Is the activity people-oriented, and is the ratio of people to space high? 2. Will it open to the street, open spaces or pathways, focusing outside to the public rather than being hidden away? 3. Are there views inside and enticement to enter (i.e. an artist's studio *with* a gallery, a workshop *with* a display room)? 4. Will the activity recognize the particular opportunities of location, ambiance and water access, and be different from those found elsewhere in the city? 5. Is it an activity with immediate appeal whose contribution of well-being can be sensed directly by a wide range of people? 6. Will the owners or directors be present on the island, to provide a sense of daily involvement in its activities? 7. Will the activity see extended use beyond the typical 9 to 5 day? 8. Does it have a high spin-off use for other activities in terms of use and image? 9. Are the people involved interested in becoming part of the community? 10. Are the space needs small, to allow for diversity and hence opportunity? 11. Are tenant applicants interested in participation rather than merely the provision of services or goods? 12. Does the activity allow for direct public-participation? 13. Is there some "fun" in the idea?

Urban design elements

While no individual reconstruction on Granville Island is a design masterpiece, the overall project concept is a real architectural accomplishment. This is due largely to five key urban design elements established at the outset by the urban designers. First, the traditional separation of pedestrians and automobiles by means of roads and sidewalks was abandoned. Instead, all circulation areas are paved with a handsomely designed concrete brick, allowing cars and pedestrians to intermingle. The interesting results are that drivers are extremely cautious and courteous on the island, small areas that would normally be wasted serve for additional parking, and pedestrians are not confined to narrow sidewalks but instead feel that the entire island is theirs. Second, the entire periphery of the island is unobstructed and a pedestrian walkway was developed to enable visitors to appreciate the unique setting. Indeed, many people are drawn to the island for the sole purpose of walking along the waterfront rather than for the commercial attractions offered. Third, a system of pipes in strong colors supported by heavy timber poles runs between the buildings and through the open spaces and serves as a powerful unifying element. These pipes also house the street lighting and provide support for canvas canopies to protect pedestrians from Vancouver's rainy climate. Fourth, the continued use of the two traditional cladding materials on the island—stucco and corrugated sheet metal—are major contributors to the unified character of the development. Fifth, to add interest and excitement to the project, the designers insisted on different colors for almost every building. Strong colors, traditionally associated with industry, were specified.

Role of the developer

One of the most important aspects of this project is the role played by the federal government through Canada Mortgage and Housing Corporation and the commitment made by the government to the project's success. Traditionally, government has been involved with development only in a regulatory manner. It is very rare that government does take the entrepreneurial initiative to create a project which will eventually stimulate further development through private investment. Granville Island's success even at this early stage indicates that some new directions in the involvement of government might be in order. Although large sums of public funds have been spent on this development, they certainly have been well spent. It may therefore be just as important for different levels of government to study this project as it is for architects and developers.

An attractive feature of Granville Island is the boat houses located on its northern shore (right). The island has extensive moorage facilities for small boats and a number of dockside restaurants. Wharf areas, with few exceptions, are accessible to the public, and as much of the Island's perimeter as possible is being developed as linear open space for walking, cycling and jogging. The streets which crisscross the island are shared by cars and pedestrians (sketch above). Motorists drive carefully and pedestrians feel that they have the run of the place.

2

Old buildings upon which care and love are lavished in the process of saving and recycling them are often important landmarks. They may be noteworthy for their historical associations, for their architectural beauty, for the value of the functions they serve — often for all three. Because seven of the eight buildings in the chapter embody such qualities, they received meticulous conservation efforts.

The Paramount Arts Centre in Aurora, Illinois, for example, formerly a movie house and now a multi-use theater for the performing arts, was and still is an Art Deco masterpiece, its ornament sensitively restored.

The St. Louis Art Museum, which houses that city's most important art collection, is a magnificent work of art in its own right. Completed in 1904 by the great American architect Cass Gilbert, it is one of this country's major Beaux Arts buildings. During the three decades in which such eclectic buildings were held in low regard, the Museum suffered many inept remodelings. Its intrinsic architectural character has now been restored by Hardy Holzman Pfeiffer Associates.

Another even more neglected landmark museum, the Arts and Industries Building of the Smithsonian Institution in Washington, DC has been brought back to its Victorian splendour by architect Hugh Jacobsen to serve as a museum for Victoriana; and a great Victorian botanical conservatory for the New York Botanical Garden has been restored by Edward Larrabee Barnes.

The first of the four buildings just mentioned has changed over time from an early movie palace, whose designers looked backward just sufficiently to provide stage room for the last throes of vaudeville, to today's new theater devoted entirely to live performance. The remaining three have been adapted and upgraded so that they can better serve their original and continuing functions as exhibition structures.

The final arts building of landmark quality included in this chapter is the Old Federal Courts Building in St. Paul. Built in 1902 for judges,

CIVIC AND CULTURAL BUILDINGS

lawyers, defendants, witnesses, and juries, it served them well until a transformation, begun in 1973, welcomed new occupants from the world of art. Now a cultural center, it has a 250-seat auditorium, shops, restaurants, and art galleries. Several of the old courtrooms, now empty stages, have been restored for their historic and architectural interest.

Another courts building in the landmark category, which still remains a court of law, is the Livingston County Courthouse in Howell, Michigan. It has been carefully restored to its original 1889 character, after having been substantially disfigured by a succession of insensitive modernizations. And the Arizona Biltmore, designed by Albert McArthur—influenced by Frank Lloyd Wright—and partially destroyed by fire, has been restored in some sections, remodeled in others, and even subjected to additions, all the better to serve its original and unchanging use as a luxurious resort hotel.

The Madison Civic Center by Hardy Holzman and Pfeiffer is the only project in this chapter which did not begin as a landmark to be saved or conserved. The Civic Center's two buildings adapted for new uses were a former movie house and a department store of no particular architectural quality. Woven together by new circulation areas, a restaurant, shops, and office space, the entire ensemble has become a highly successful arts complex which includes a multi-purpose performing arts facility, an experimental theater, and an art gallery. Preserved in this dramatic transformation has been the small neighborly scale of the commercial sector of downtown Madison, Wisconsin—nice, but not of landmark quality either.

The lesson to be learned from the Madison Civic Center is a new one. Landmarks are not the only buildings worth saving. More of the built world than we now may think must be renewed and reused. Maybe almost all of it.

1
THE NEW MADISON CIVIC CENTER
BY HARDY HOLZMAN PFEIFFER ASSOCIATES

What have we here? What sort of facade is this? What will Malcolm Holzman think of next? Is it Post Modernist? Is it a quotation from late twenties Hispano-Moorish movie palace kitsch? Is it a quotation at all? Can it be the entire text? Or even the real thing—a genuine old cinema palace—phoenix? And now multipurpose? It is indeed the latter, the entrance facade left almost intact except for minor refurbishment including cleaning and repointing the brick and installing the ''dumb and ordinary'' new doorway; and the interior restored and adapted for a wide range of musical and theatrical performance.

To the left and right of the portal are symmetrical infilled walls that screen the new expanded facilities which replace former

structures torn down. The windows in these walls are staggered in height, building toward the crown of the niche in the upper portal—a gesture toward the niche and the elaborate Spanish Baroque cornice, and to the five Spanish Romanesque windows that form a curve in the portal recess.

Connected to an infilled wall but down the street and out of the range of the camera lens is another unabashed facade, its masonry also clean and newly pointed. This one is more or less Georgian and was formerly the front of a Montgomery Ward department store built in 1941. And the old store? It is now the art museum of the Civic Center.

Neither of the two fronts are or ever were considered to be much as architecture

(the Chicago firm of movie theater architects Rapp and Rapp had built grander facades for more sumptuous movie palaces and the storefront was designed by the Montgomery Ward engineering department). Their restoration by HHPA has been modest and low key in keeping with the scale and feeling of the small commercial buildings along both sides of the street. These facades, then, are neither arcane Post Modernist quotations nor landmarks in their own right. Nothing much has been done to them. Why pay attention?

Because these humble fixed-up fronts and the pedestrian mall they face are the only visible signs on the main street of Madison, Wisconsin of the existence behind them of a $7.5 million civic and cultural center which,

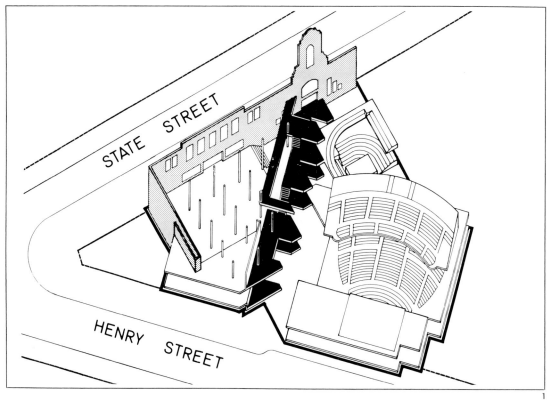

The site (1) is two blocks from Madison's most beautiful building and important landmark, the State Capitol (2), and six blocks from the main campus of the University of Wisconsin at the opposite end of the State Street axis (3). The project forms a major element in a downtown revitalization plan, which includes the State Street Transit/Mall for pedestrians and buses developed by M. Paul Friedberg & Partners and new commercial, office and residential development. Both the State Street (above) and Henry Street facades (7, 8) combine elements of new and existing construction. On State Street the buildings on either side of the old Capitol Theater facade have been removed, along with the marquee and metal display cases. A shot-sawn limestone entry has been installed to complement the buff brick and decorative terra cotta of the Hispano-Moorish facade of the old movie house, and new exterior infill walls have surfaces of bull-nose and flat oversized brick in good scale with the ornament of the remaining buildings.

2

3

4

5

6

7

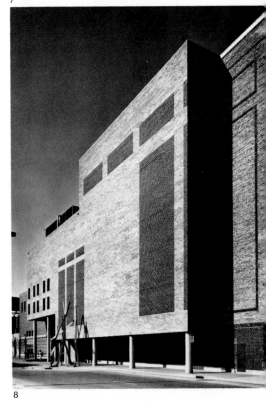

8

since it opened last February, is already bringing new vitality to Madison's steadily reviving downtown. And even more importantly because architects Hugh Hardy, Malcolm Holzman and Norman Pfeiffer seem to be saying that the forms and ornament of buildings have no intrinsic meaning but gain their signification through the way the buildings are used. Thus these styles, however disparate, and despite the ideas and feelings they have symbolized in the past will gain a new resonance. They will come to speak of a lively public interest in the arts as surely as the Neo-Classic forms of Madison's famous State Capitol building (2) have long signified the powers of law and government.

Not everyone would agree. Traditionally communities have built large and elegant buildings to attest to their commitment to the arts. "Make no small plans," said Daniel Burnham and Frank Lloyd Wright would have concurred. Wright, buried near Madison at Taliesin in Spring Green, believed that his city should have built its auditorium and civic center on Lake Monona, one of the city's two huge lakes. Said Wright to the local Eagles Club in 1939: "There isn't enough civic spirit in Madison to do something great, regardless of who wins or loses or whose ox is gored. Why not wake up, go places, do something with the beautiful site Nature gave you."

There were more than a few civic leaders, however, who shared Wright's dream of magnificence for Madison. In 1955 they asked him to design the great Monona Terrace project, modifications of which by the Taliesin Fellowship were under consideration until 1974 when lack of public support, extensive litigation and a major shift in city planning concepts caused the project to be permanently shelved.

The realization that the Monona Terrace project was too grandiose for a small city like Madison came gradually, but was spurred on by the fact that its downtown was dying. People began to see that not only was the project too big, it was in the wrong place as well. In 1974 in response to the advice of the Madison City Planning Department and the urgings of its assistant planning director, John A. Urich, the city's then new mayor, Paul Soglin, purchased the old Capitol Theater and the empty Montgomery Ward department store on State Street to be recycled into the long desired civic center. Soglin, now replaced by a new mayor, considers this to have been one of the most important single actions he took during his six-year term of office. "Just the fact that what we have now is on State Street," says Soglin, "that it holds together the community, business and educational functions of the city and is available to pedestrian traffic is a different concept for

9

11

The thrust theater, known as the Isthmus Playhouse, seats 370 people in a balcony and orchestra with no seat more than seven rows from the stage. This room has been designed for a diversity of productions ranging from children's theater, puppet shows and chamber music to formal drama. To accommodate such flexibility, the stage is fully trapped. The rear-stage wall is demountable in modular sections. Specially designed carpet covered benches compensate for the range of sizes of the child and adult patrons. The Madison Art Center (12) now occupies the main selling floor of the former Montgomery Ward store.

10

12

The complex has four main levels (15) interconnected with a multi-storied lobby called the Crossroads (13, 14, 16), which joins three exterior and ten interior entrances—on six levels in all. It serves the audiences of the two theaters (sometimes more than 3,000 when combined) and includes an informal theater space (14).

13

14

Madison. The thought of an art center that people can drop into in the middle of the day, without making a special trip is pivotal. The space inside the building—the open areas which are not simply corridors but can be used for performances at noon—is a recognition of the fact that people will come out during their lunch hour, eat and see a performance."

A significant building for the arts built before World War II would have been in an outlying city park. The urban renewal of the fifties and sixties also put buildings for culture into enclaves. The whole idea of weaving a major arts facility into a decaying downtown commercial fabric is what is new. According to Soglin, the new complex has already begun to enliven the surrounding area. "We managed to prevent the ghost town effect later in the day as various parts of the city close up. Because the Civic Center is near a densely populated residential section and yet is easily accessible from the downtown offices, the city is now alive after six in the evening. And the location saves gas. Drive to work in the morning, walk to a performance or an art show at the end of the day and then drive home. Or take a bus. Madison has the best bus system of any city its size in the United States. Within a few blocks of the new facility you can catch a bus to any part of the city." Soglin points out furthermore that the downtown location of the Civic Center allows the same parking facilities to be used both day and night, a plus since parking facilities take up a lot of space and are expensive to build.

Soglin also believes that the new center will strengthen Madison's ties with the University of Wisconsin. "Some of the university people were very nervous about the project because they were afraid it would rival the university's cultural programs. I think that the city facility augments what the university already has and out of this will come greater cultural growth. Town and gown are both on the State Street axis, so they tie together in the physical as well as the cultural sense."

Soglin has hopes that the new Civic Center will strengthen the State of Wisconsin's commitment to the arts. Wisconsin until two years ago had the lowest per capita allocation for the arts of any state in the U.S. "I think," says Soglin, "that we will see greater support of the Wisconsin Arts Council, which in turn will provide more funding for activities within the city and in the rest of the state. So if there is an expansion of the poet-in-the-schools program in Eau Claire, it can be attributed to the Civic Center as the central force in an effort to get the state interested in all the arts."

Architects Hardy, Holzman and Pfeiffer

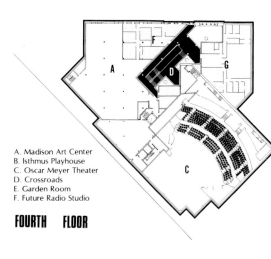

A. Madison Art Center
B. Isthmus Playhouse
C. Oscar Meyer Theater
D. Crossroads
E. Garden Room
F. Future Radio Studio

FOURTH FLOOR

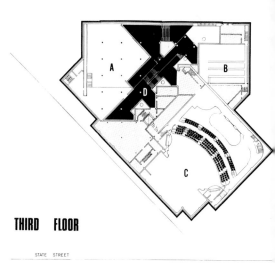

THIRD FLOOR

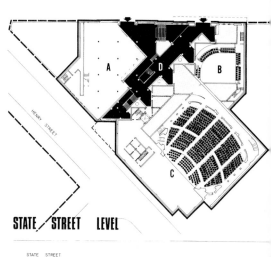

STATE STREET LEVEL

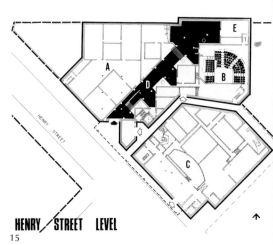

HENRY STREET LEVEL

15

17

18

19

20

21

22

hope, with their former client Soglin, that the new complex will have a far-reaching effect upon the cultural life of the state. They also hope that the success of the center will cause architects and their clients to remember that average, ordinary buildings are of value, "not because their detail is superb and fantastic," says Malcolm Holzman, but for other reasons. Holzman believes that in the 1980s and '90s architects will be dealing more and more with the problem of what to do with average buildings. "It would be easy to argue that we should tear them down because their only value is their structure and to some extent their skin. But there is a cultural attachment to old buildings, and they are part of the fabric of the city. If you remove them, how can you suitably match that fabric? And they are an important energy resource. Saving bricks represents the conservation of the energy which bricks embody. Clients ask what we know about energy conservation, but their question usually relates to solar collectors and windmills. People understand the need to insulate but when we propose to reuse a building they don't understand that as energy conservation. Or the use of energy in tearing it all down and putting it there a second time. There is an enormous expenditure of energy just in the structural frame of a building."

But Holzman also reminds us that saving and recycling old buildings is very hard and time-consuming architectural work. Now that a movie palace and a department store have been neatly interwoven together, the effort doesn't show. "But," says Holzman, "how you thread a piece of steel through a building to hold up concrete and bricks and then cover it all up so that no one knows it is there is absolutely the opposite of the structural expressionism everyone was so fond of twenty years ago. In re-use projects you don't create great stunning structural feats. You are mainly involved with little structural adjustments, which are very difficult for the contractors. Holding things up and putting things under them, that kind of thing."

Contractors who are bidding such projects have a hard time estimating from the drawings how much work there will be in recycling an old building. Sometimes it is difficult even for the architects to describe definitively how much work there is, so the situation often occurs where the contractor has not bid everything or the architects haven't drawn it. "It is a new kind of architectural performance," asserts Holzman, "but it is worth it. What we did respected the scale of that town. If we had done something new at that scale made of pieces which would have looked right with the old buildings on the street, it would have cost much more money than our renovation. If the Civic Cen-

ter had been built new in any other way, it would have looked too big. The way we saved the framework of State Street is a value that cannot be measured in dollars. The saving of the movie palace auditorium—you could never get a room like that in a new building."

Architects Hardy, Holzman and Pfeiffer are fond of Madison. "It is a wonderful city," says Holzman, "because you can still see how it began. The Capitol, the most prominent building, is located on a rise and its vistas have been preserved by zoning height regulations. As architecture it has no rival. The city has a fine stock of masonry and wood buildings. When you come to its commercial areas—State Street is one of the oldest—most of the fabric closest to the Capitol is still intact and consists of small stores 20 to 30 feet wide and each one owned by an independent entrepreneur. As you move down State Street toward the University this fabric becomes eroded somewhat because of the growth in the sixties. The buildings which look out of place in Madison are the new big ones and the University built most of them."

The architects also like Madison's town plan laid out on a grid system in 1836 by a Federal judge and real estate speculator, James Duane Doty. Within the grid which runs between Lake Monona and Lake Mendota is the Capitol, from which four avenues extend to the north, south, east and west creating in effect a rotated grid. Each avenue cuts the grid at a 45 degree angle creating a number of triangulated lots of which the Civic Center site is one. Everyone familiar with the plans of Hardy Holzman Pfeiffer Associates knows they like to work with rotated squares forming triangulations. "If we hadn't had them we would of course have invented them," said Holzman, "but this time they were built in."

MADISON CIVIC CENTER, Madison, Wisconsin. Owner: The City of Madison. Architects: *Hardy Holzman Pfeiffer Associates—partner-in-charge: Malcolm Holzman; supervising architect: Theron E. Grinage;* HHPA team: *Conrad Schaub, Perry Hall, William Jordan, Victor Gong, Bun-Wah Nip, Robert York, Dorothy Alexander, Michel Lewis, James DeSpirito, Neil Dixon, Jan Gorlach;* project representatives: *Peter Blossom, Duane Hinz.* Engineers: *Ketchum Barrett Nickel Austin/Besier* (structural); *Mechanical Design, Inc.* (mechanical/electrical). Consultants: *Jaffe Acoustics, Inc.* (acoustical); *Jules Fisher Associates* (theater lighting); *Jules Fisher & Paul Marantz* (special lighting); *Theater Techniques, Incorporated* (stage); *Boyce Nemec Designs* (projection & equipment); *George D. Cattabiani* (elevator); *Dennis Pearson* (stained glass); *Morrison/Hannah Designs* (Isthmus Playhouse seating). General contractor: *Orville E. Madsen & Son, Inc.*

23

The old Capitol Theater (17–22) has been completely refinished: all plaster surfaces are now restored and painted with stencils in 14 different values and finishes (27, 28). The colors have been selected to produce special effects in combination with a new three-color house lighting system, which includes the newly illuminated ceiling coves of the original movie house (23, 24, 25). New aisle carpeting has been rewoven from the original design and the new draperies are in complementary colors. Two large chandeliers (26) have been fashioned from five small existing ones (21).

24

25

Adapting a movie theatre for multi-purpose activities

The following check list indicates the three major areas—stage, audience and technical—that need consideration in determining the suitability of using an old movie theater as a multipurpose hall. Each item indicates: 1) how movie theaters were constructed; 2) today's requirements: and 3) changes made to the former Capitol Theater in Madison, Wisconsin. It was prepared by HHPA with Paul Marantz, Bernard Weiss, Boyce Nemec, Christopher Jaffe and Robert Davis.

STAGE REQUIREMENTS

Size
1. Most movie-theater stages constructed prior to 1930 were 50 to 80 feet wide but at most 20 to 30 feet deep.
2. Today, requirements for a 70- to 100-piece orchestra, ballet company or Broadway show necessitate a minimum of 35 or up to 60 feet of depth for grand opera.
3. The existing rear stage wall of the Capitol Theater was removed and reconstructed to provide an expanded stage depth of 35 feet.

Orchestra pit
1. Orchestra pits in old movie theaters permitted a maximum of 20 to 30 musicians, and seldom extended below or behind the front edge of the stage.
2. Many of today's productions require 40 musicians (60 to 80 for opera).
3. The existing fixed pit of the Capitol Theater, 48 feet by 8 feet, and four rows of orchestra seating were removed. They were replaced by a 56- by 20-foot hydraulic pit lift. It stops at four levels: basement for loading, 5 ft-6 in. below orchestra seating to serve as a musicians' area, orchestra seating level to augment capacity with four rows of removable seats, and stage level to assist in loading/unloading and for certain productions to increase stage size.

Stagehouses
1. These were usually built to the side and rear property lines of the old movie houses. Included within this space were the firestair and dressing rooms.
2. Today, off-stage space for the movement of performers (especially dance) and scenery is a necessity.
3. For the re-cycled Capitol Theater, 1,900 square feet of wing space were added stage left for movement of performers and scenery and to accommodate star dressing rooms.

Dressing rooms
1. Most old movie theaters had 10 to 20 dressing rooms, which accommodated 2 to 4 people starting one level above the stage and running the full height of the stage tower.
2. The dressing rooms most in demand now are at stage level for use by stars and their entourage. These usually include private bathrooms. Next in demand are chorus dressing rooms accommodating 20 to 40 people.
3. Two 100-square-foot dressing rooms with toilets were constructed at the Capitol's stage level.

Two chorus dressing rooms totaling 1,500 square feet were constructed one level below the stages.

Green Room, warm-up rooms, rehearsal rooms
1. These were rarely included in old movie theaters.
2. Today they are in demand by resident companies and touring groups.
3. As part of the transformation of the Capitol Theater, a 1900-square-foot rehearsal room was constructed with a professional dance floor. A Green Room and warm-up room were not provided.

Construction shops and storage
1. These facilities were never included in movie theaters.
2. Today, resident companies require them for the production and storage of sets and costumes.
3. None are provided for the new theater.

Loading facilities
1. These were usually minimal. Movie theater stages were often served by the same stage door used by performers.
2. In today's multipurpose hall they are crucial to a successful operation. If scenery, sets, costumes, instruments, etc., cannot be loaded in and out within a few hours, many touring companies will not agree to perform.
3. A new series of 8- by 10-foot acoustical loading doors have been installed with direct access to the pit lift. An 80-square-foot elevator also services the stage from the street level.

Administration
1. These spaces were rarely more than minimal.
2. For live performances today, these areas grow in number to include: public relations, accounting, bookings, ushers, etc.
3. 1900 square feet of new administrative office space was constructed in the new facility.

AUDIENCE REQUIREMENTS

Seating
1. The 1920s and '30s provided us with movie theater seats that were generally 18 to 20 inches wide, with back-to-back spacing of 30 inches.
2. Now most communities demand 20- to 22-inch-wide seats; back-to-back measure of comfort is 34 to 36 inches. These dimensions can usually be accommodated with a reduction in the number of seats in the orchestra level, but not in the stepped balconies or loges.
3. In the renovated Capitol, the new seats are 34 inches back-to-back and the individual seats are wider. There are now fewer seats in the orchestra and more in the balcony. The theater capacity has not been appreciably changed.

Lobby
1. Lobbies in downtown and neighborhood movie theaters vary in size, but function primarily as a place to hold some patrons waiting between continuous shows.
2. For live performance a lobby must comfortably accommodate all of the patrons prior to performance, during intermission, and may also have to function as a place for community events.
3. For the Madison Civic Center, a new lobby, the Crossroads, was constructed with light and sound locks servicing all theater levels. It includes an informal performance place, refreshment areas, box office, and coat room.

Box office
1. Box offices of older theaters were usually just large enough for two people dispensing tickets to one performance.

2. The box office of today's multipurpose hall sell tickets to many performances, sometimes months in advance. Many are computerized and directly involved with administrative functions.

3. A new four-position box office and subscription area with computer consoles was installed in the new facility.

Toilet facilities

1,2. Building codes change and so have the public demands for these facilities.

3. New men's and women's toilets were constructed on four different levels.

TECHNICAL REQUIREMENTS

Rigging

1. Movie theaters were equipped with stage rigging to meet the requirements of vaudeville: A hemp-type system with a pinrail at stage level, with several special wire-guided counterweight sets for border lights, picture screen, screen masking, a house traveler track with curtain and a fire curtain.

2. Production requirements for theater or opera include a counterweight rigging system with sets on 6 in. centers capable of handling 800- to 1000-pound loads. A loading bridge should also be provided. Fly galleries should be on both sides of the stage with pinrails to handle spot lines and special rigging.

3. A new counterweight system with sets on 6 in. centers was installed at the Madison Civic Center for the full stage depth in addition to fly galleries, grid, pinrails, etc.

House lighting

1. Movie theater lighting was atmospheric—designed to create moods.

2. Requirements for seeing in a multipurpose hall far exceed those conditions suitable for motion pictures. Supplementary lighting must allow patrons to read printed programs, identify reserved-seat numbers, and mingle during intermission. Modern electronic dimming systems can replace the complex mechanical systems previously used to achieve color blending and dynamic light transitions, and recall them with a touch of a button.

3. A new three-color cove lighting system, refabricated chandeliers, refurbished wall sconces, aisle lights and new downlights were installed at the Madison Civic Center.

Stage lighting

1. Most existing lighting equipment in movie houses is located on stage and has seen 50 years of diminishing use.

2. Power requirements in a multipurpose facility are many times that of the original equipment. As much as 30 per cent of a stage-lighting system, including its control, is located on the audience side of the proscenium. Adequate space must be found for new equipment that is accessible for maintenance, esthetically compatible with the auditorium decor and located in the correct relationship and distance to the stage.

3. No lighting equipment was recoverable from the original Capitol Theater. The new installation includes: memory control console, patch panels, dimmer and relay racks. Stage lighting in the auditorium has been mounted on two pairs of ladders adjacent to the proscenium, placed on extensions to the front of the balcony, mounted above the ceiling and in the follow spot booth.

Acoustics

1. Movie theaters were not designed to strict acoustical parameters for live performances, although they did accommodate a variety of musical and speech presentations ranging from organ music accompanying a silent film to an occassional vaudeville soprano.

2. Movie theaters vary in their physical layout but their volumes are often similar to those specified today for opera houses. These spaces do not usually have sufficient reverberation for symphonic use and fan-shaped spaces do not provide adequate reflection to the central orchestra area. Consideration must be given to the types of performances to be housed, whether the acoustical criteria will be achieved by the introduction of electronic or natural sound-reinforcement systems. Today's productions require sophisticated communication systems; actor call, program monitoring, audience call, expanded control-room facilities and in-house mixing.

3. The stage tower volume of the Capitol Theater was physically coupled to the house through a curtain, and a lightweight articulated shell was designed to blend and balance orchestral sound, improve distribution of the harmonic structure, and assist the musicians in hearing themselves and others. The pit was enlarged and acoustically designed for an opera orchestra. An extensive theater sound system was installed to add to the room's natural acoustics. A main cluster of speakers was located behind a sound-transparent proscenium drapery supplemented with under balcony speakers. The basic system is designed for speech, jazz and musical theater only. Extensive additional power and conduit systems were installed to allow highly amplified groups to rapidly assemble their own touring systems in the theater.

Film

1, 2. Most movie-theater prosceniums can accommodate the range of current and traditional film formats from the early 1:1.33 height-to-width ratio to the wide screen 1:2.25 images.

In some large movie theaters, the projection down-angle to the screen was extreme, 18 degrees. Today's standards to reduce distortion and provide sharp focus over the entire image are not more than six degrees. Technological improvements in equipment no longer restrict the size of the displayed image. Instead the image size is controlled by the comfortable (20 degrees) upward viewing angle from the front seat and the cut-off line of the balcony from the last orchestra seat.

3. The existing movie equipment of the Capitol Theater has been fully refurbished to conform with Academy standards. A new suspended screen and sound system has been installed.

Mechanical system

1. The early theaters employed ventilation as a means of removing heat. Air was generally drawn into the building through the basement, forced up vents below the seats, exiting through perforations in the ceiling and attic space. Improvements to this basic convection system included employing fans, introduction of heat and finally cooling.

2. The problems of environmental room control in the modern auditorium are complex: an audience will not tolerate more than a 5 degree temperature differential during a performance; humidity control is essential to audience comfort and acoustics: energy-conservation requires reuse of air where possible; and live performance power-requirements create large amounts of heat to be dissipated.

3. All mechanical systems at the Madison Civic Center have been replaced to meet today's energy requirements and conservation guidelines. Shafts, ducts, and chases have been reused where possible.

28

Robert C. Lautman photos

2
EVOKING THE SPIRIT OF 1876 FOR A DISPLAY OF VICTORIANA

The Arts and Industries Building of the Smithsonian Institution was begun in 1879 and opened soon after. With guidance from the Smithsonian's architectural and engineering staff and consulting architect Hugh Newell Jacobsen, the great but tragically neglected old building was renewed for the Bicentennial. The museum's curators installed an entirely new exhibition of Victorian artifacts, some of which were originally shown to commemorate the nation's 100th birthday at the famous 1876 Exposition in Philadelphia. The exhibition has been designed less to teach about the past than to give the experience of having been in it. Its great popular success owes much to the behind-the-scenes work of Jacobsen, who elected not to attempt a literal restoration of the interiors, but to recapture the essence of their late-19th-century expression.

The budget permitted the restoration of only one of the Arts and Industries Building's four facades, and the front entry (above) was the logical choice. The work included cleaning and renewing the ornamentation, replacing damaged brick in the vestibule and installing a new set of oak and walnut doors (right). The old photograph (left) served as one of the references for the exterior restoration.

The "exposition" as an idea is a 19th century phenomenon originating in the desire on the part of government and industry to inform and excite the public about technological and industrial advance. So important culturally were these exhibits devoted to the products of industry, that the most important of them gave a name to and thus helped define the style of the time. Until the end of the 19th century, styles were named after kings, emperors and an occasional queen. Now, most classifiers in the fields of 19th and 20th century architecture and the fine and decorative arts will, wherever possible, label the design of a period with the name of its most important exhibition. Thus we have the style of the Paris Exposition Universelle of 1900, which has its roots in some of the artifacts shown in London's Great Exhibition of 1851 held in Joseph Paxton's Crystal Palace. In the United States, the revival of neo-classicism was heralded by the Chicago World's Fair of 1893.

Less famous but of great cultural importance, nonetheless, was the 1876 Exposition in Philadelphia's Fairmont Park. No previous fair had so effectively presented the growing inventive genius of the United States. The Arts and Industries Building in Washington, D.C. was originally constructed by the Smithsonian to house box car loads of objects from this exposition, which had been transported from Philadelphia by steam engine and dumped on the Mall. (Most of these artifacts were eventually discarded). In 1976, in honor of the Bicentennial, the Smithsonian used the Arts and Industries Building as the setting for an exhibition that evokes the spirit of the 1876 Centennial. The show includes approximately 25,-000 objects of this period, 15 per cent of which are actually from the Centennial Exposition.

A careful restoration of the Arts and Industries Building was long overdue and the installation of the Bicentennial exhibit made it essential. Before Victorian structures began to re-emerge as objects of beauty and curiosity, the Arts and Industries Building had been treated with contempt, in part because of the ascendance of the neo-classic style launched at the 1893 Chicago World's Fair just noted. Even when it opened, in 1881, it had not been thought very much of in spite of the fact that it was the first government building to be electrified. It had the misfortune of having been built cheaply (for $3.20 per square foot) and was indeed Washington's most inexpensively constructed public building. Designed by Adolph Cluss and Rudolph Schulze, who had been doing schools, it was their first major structure, and they rigorously kept costs down. Cruciform in plan with four similar facades, it has no basement and an open steel joist ceiling. Except for the central rotunda and the four entrance halls, which were laid in encaustic tile, most of the floors were originally of wood.

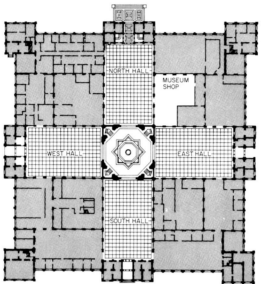

The drawing above shows the west hall as it appeared in 1881, the year the Arts and Industries Building opened. The occasion was the Inaugural Ball for President James Garfield. The balconies that appear in the recent photo (opposite page) were added around 1910. The design of the new stencils over the arches is similar to those in the drawing and were based upon careful study of old photographs with a jeweler's loupe. The plan (left) is current, and shows a Victorian fountain, added by Jacobsen, where a fountain always should have been, but never was before. All of the artifacts (below and right) have been painted and shined to look like new.

Early records indicate that the building was exceedingly uncomfortable. In the first nine years, ten Smithsonian employees died of influenza and the damp wood floors laid on grade were blamed. These floors were gradually replaced with marble tiles.

In the 95 years that elapsed between the first opening day and the spring of 1976, the fine old building had been altered many times, but never until 1976 in a way which even observed, much less enhanced, its true esthetic qualities. Because of his successful restoration for the Smithsonian of the Renwick, architect Hugh Jacobsen was commissioned by Paul N. Perrot, Assistant Secretary for Museum Programs, to deal with the now recognized esthetic and stylistic aspects of the most recent remodeling. Meanwhile the in-house Office of Facilities Planning and Engineering Services was hard at work solving the general problems connected with heating, ventilating, air conditioning and upgrading the physical fabric of the structure.

Jacobsen began by considering and then dismissing the question as to which of its many past guises the interior should be restored, because the interiors had never been decorated in a unified style. "They had hacks back then too," says he, "and they made mistakes." No single interior renovation, as examined in old (1880-1890) photographs with the aid of a jeweler's loupe seemed just right to Jacobsen, but some of the details did, including the encaustic tile floor, already mentioned, which had been removed and discarded except for the west entry hall. The problem as Jacobsen saw it was to select, assemble and reproduce only those details which best evoked the spirit of the Victorian structure. A literal restoration of the interiors as they appeared at any one time would not only have been prohibitive in cost, but also an esthetic disaster.

A comparison of the photographs of the renovation with early photographs (far left and below right) indicates that Jacobsen's approach was successful. Although he did not design the exhibition itself (this was done by the Arts and Industries Building's curatorial staff), Jacobsen and his project architect, Paul B. Pavlovich, were responsible for the stenciling, flooring, hardware, colors, fenestration, doors, graphics and lighting (other than the hanging chandeliers). The interior colors match samples discovered under seven or eight layers of paint. The colors of the stenciling were selected in the same manner with the aid of extensive reading of contemporary correspondence in the Smithsonian Institution archives.

ARTS AND INDUSTRIES BUILDING, Washington, D.C. Owner: *The Smithsonian Institution.* Architect: *Hugh Newell Jacobsen—Paul B. Pavlovich* (project architect); associated architects: *The Smithsonian Institution, Office of Facilities Planning and Engineering Services, Engineering and Design Branch— William L. Thomas* (architect-in-charge). General contractor: *Grunley-Walsh Construction Co., Inc.* Principal subcontractors: *H. & R. Johnson, Inc.* (ceramic tile fabricator); *Standard Art Marble and Tile Co.* (tile installer); *Myers-Christiansen Co.* (wall stencilwork).

The old photograph (left) was made on a glass negative, now cracked. It shows the original encaustic tile floor in the central rotunda, and the decorated frieze below the dome. The photos (above and at right) show the new Jacobsen designed stencils, the newly installed Victorian fountain, and the new encaustic tile floor. The process of duplicating the old tile floor was a formidable one. Determining the exact sizes, shapes and color was difficult as Jacobsen and his team had only a half dozen or so original photos to work from. Finding the source for the encaustic tile was particularly difficult since the method of producing it had been universally abandoned in the mid-thirties. Enquiries were sent to almost all tile firms in the United States, Europe and Mexico. Only two firms were willing to experiment with encaustic tile production, and after one year of these experiments, the job was given to H & R Johnson, Inc., in Great Britain, who are the successors to the firm which laid the original tiles in the Arts and Industries Building. In brief, the re-discovered process consists of stamping a so-called "green" tile with a patterned die, firing it, filling the depressed area with one or more pigmented clays and refiring it.

3
HARDY HOLZMAN PFEIFFER RE-ESTABLISH THE FORMAL THEMES OF A GREAT BEAUX ARTS BUILDING

Cass Gilbert was the original architect of the St. Louis Art Museum completed in 1904. Like other American Beaux Arts architects he looked to ancient Rome in his search for the timeless architectural values which he hoped to bring to his work. For his vast St. Louis project, designed as part of the St. Louis Exposition, he decided that the Thermae of Caracalla had a spatial order which would be just right. (A few years later McKim, Mead and White were to turn to the same source for Pennsylvania Station). He fashioned the combined concourse and sculpture hall of the museum (right and overleaf) after the tepidarium. As in the Roman bath, the hall has three great bays with arched recesses at opposite ends of each bay. The whole is roofed by a barrel vault interrupted by lunettes. At each end of the main axis are three arched doorways spanned by a balcony and crowned by a lunette. All of these elements, thanks to the perceptions and craft of Hugh Hardy, Malcolm Holzman and Norman Pfeiffer have become readable once more and a magnificent room has emerged. The architects, who call what they do "interpretive restoration," have also re-discovered and sucessfully restated the formal dynamics of other spaces within the museum. They clearly love the building. In Hugh Hardy's words: "This major work by a once-forgotten architect gives delight in its audacity and solidity, its remembrance of the past and its commitment to the future."

Through the 74-year life of the museum, Cass Gilbert's design was little understood, and many depredations were made upon it (top and left). HHP began by removing these piecemeal accretions, thus re-stating Gilbert's axial and spatial themes. The main axis (overleaf) and the minor axis (opposite page) were clarified and enhanced. The museum insisted that the fountain at the crossing of the two axes remain and the architects agreed. Though not part of Cass Gilbert's original design, it helps turn the concourse from a channel to a room. By making the most of the fountain, HHP had all of architectural and town planning wisdom behind them, for every intersection of paths of movement is transformed by a monument or fountain as a place to stop and be.

The architects investigated Gilbert's ornament and color palettes in buildings in which they were better preserved than in the art museum (the St. Louis Public library for an example). They found that he loved bright colors and rich decorative devices. The Sculpture Hall once had a highly patterned tile ceiling. Despite what they learned, HHP elected to use color and ornament sparingly in the belief that color and decoration of extreme subtlety was better suited to today's esthetic standards. The over-all effect has the delicacy in color and light of a fine drawing in the Beaux Arts manner.

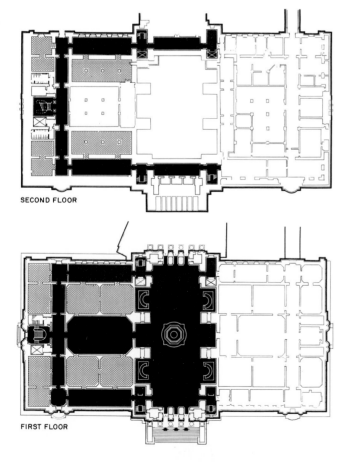

SECOND FLOOR

FIRST FLOOR

Cass Gilbert's axes form a lattice of movement which surrounds and contains the exhibition spaces. Down through the years, no one seems to have understood the architectural significance of this lattice or how it worked. Museum curators who should have known better cluttered these passages, blocked them off, sealed their windows and created fake period environments for their genuine art—making it difficult to distinguish between the two (top and left).

In order to re-establish the lattice, HHP had to cut new openings in certain walls and restore existing doorways and frames. All the openings and walls in the transformed main floor areas have new moldings copied from Gilbert's own profiles. The architects elected to restore this much of the ornament to introduce elements of appropriate scale within the huge volumes of the rooms. Doorways less grand than these would have looked hopelessly forlorn.

Where necessary the elegant doorways contain smoke alarm-activated, roll-down fire doors. These doors are carefully integrated into the delicately molded frames. Their presence is revealed by a nearly concealed one inch slot in the head and jambs.

The vista at right is a view from the Sculpture Hall, through a principal gallery to the hall containing the main staircase beyond. The gallery for smaller sculpture (below left) is parallel to the main facade.

The gallery (below right) has casework and moldings by Gilbert and murals by Elmer Garnsey. This square, domed room is lit by an oculus (not shown).

Cass Gilbert's skylights (section below) were re-constructed, re-glazed and augmented by incandescent light. The quantity of daylight was greatly reduced and the combined light better directed to the lower or viewing portions of the walls. The museum was not originally designed for electric light, but an early incandescent system (above) was temporarily put in place for the 1904 St. Louis Exposition.

The museum required a new grand staircase (right) which HHP executed in an altogether contemporary manner. Nonetheless, by its sinuous curve, and dark rich colors it makes a gesture toward Gilbert's classicism.

A gallery on the second floor, one of two skylit studios which Gilbert had designed as places to give art classes, was used for storage (left) until this restoration. It is now the major new gallery for the display of prints, drawings and photographs (below). Its skylight has been reglazed with two layers of solar glass and fitted with louver blinds.

All wall surfaces throughout the renovation upon which paintings are hung have been resurfaced with 32-ply birch plywood, a surface easily repaired after the removal of paintings.

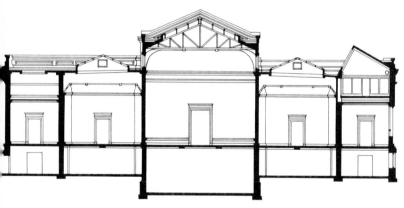

There are not many architects still alive who received Beaux Arts training before 1930—the date which marks the ending of the influence of the Ecole des Beaux Arts in the United States. In the last four decades, those among them who believed that the birth of the Modern Movement heralded the death of true Architecture were little heeded when they spoke with admiration of the work of Henry Hornbostel, Stanford White, Paul Cret, John Russell Pope, Ralph Adams Cram, Bertram Goodhue, Cass Gilbert and the rest.

The few older architects who are still around to enjoy watching the younger practitioners discover Goodhue and Gilbert must also envy them their opportunities to restore fine eclectic buildings—chances these same young architects are eagerly seizing.

During the thirties, forties, fifties and sixties in the United States most alterations or additions to beautiful old buildings were depredations performed by architects for whom the eclectic work had little meaning or value. Today, more of the public, more owners, and more architects value our heritage of buildings which predate the Modern Movement and contemporary architectural styles. And more architects—through their historical and theoretical studies which are today's substitutes for Beaux Arts training—have begun to understand the formal dynamics of the historical styles.

This is a hopeful sign. Much critical attention is now being paid to the influences of a given architect's historical and theoretical understanding upon his original creative work. Just as important, however, is the influence of this understanding upon the buildings and urban environments which he is now being invited to repair or transform.

Today, because of energy concerns, the cost of new buildings, and the heightened awareness of the value of our architectural heritage, many architects get more invitations to fix an old building than to build a new one. A grand old state capitol, court house, post office, library or museum that needs a new roof usually also needs air conditioning, new plumbing and wiring and improved lighting.

Often this is all the client wants, but if the building is of architectural quality, the good architect tries to do more. He raises the level of dialogue with his client by helping him discover the building's timeless formal values, persuading him to restore these too. Another dialogue must then begin between the architect who will restore and the predecessor who designed a building with the strength to survive its own time.

Hugh Hardy, the partner-in-charge of the $6.6 million St. Louis restoration, immersed himself in the life and work of Cass Gilbert. Though he was one of America's most famous Beaux Arts architects, Gilbert never studied at the Ecole des Beaux Arts. He died in 1934 at the age of seventy-four. He was then what we call today an establishment figure, helping found the Architectural League in 1881, serving as its president, and becoming the president of the AIA. For good measure he served as president of the National Academy of Design and as a trustee of the Metropolitan Museum of Art.

His fame barely outlasted his life, for as a leading eclectic he was to be ignored by the polemicists of the Modern Movement who began to be heard in the decade of his death, and this eclipse of his reputation demonstrates the exclusionary power of polemic. Gilbert had, after all, designed the Woolworth Building (once the world's tallest) and the United States Custom House in New York, the United States Supreme Court Building in Washington, D.C., the St. Louis Public Library, in 1933 an arts building for Oberlin College (made famous once more because of a highly controversial addition by Robert Venturi), and many other commercial, institutional and governmental buildings.

Hugh Hardy believes that many of these projects established an eminent style which was widely copied. A re-assessment of Gilbert's work would help illuminate a period that the historians have neglected for too long. HHP's brilliant restoration of the St. Louis Art Museum should instigate the process.

The museum began as an integral part of a much grander scheme which Gilbert composed for the 1904 Exposition. It became a freestanding permanent masonry building displaying U.S. painting and plaster casts of sculpture as part of the Fair's complex devoted to the fine arts. During the Fair it was surrounded by temporary stucco pavilions displaying the art of Great Britain, Germany, Holland, Belgium, Italy and France. These temporary pavilions were later removed.

Although, as already noted, the art museum derives the form of its main hall from the Thermae of Caracalla, its galleries are not spanned by Roman masonry vaults. Gilbert made the most of the techniques available to him at the time and roofed his vast skylit galleries with steel trusses, using industrial building techniques.

Many neo-classic museums built around the turn of the century are composed in a manner similar to St. Louis with lower exhibition halls symmetrically arranged on opposite sides of a high vaulted central hall. Hardy points out, however, that "although Gilbert's spatial arrangement cannot be called unique, it is remarkably subtle in the way a variety of skylit volumes manipulates natural light. It is these contrasts between a central 38-foot-tall

composition because they understand it themselves

gallery and others of 24 feet and 18 feet—some on the north, some on the south, some with clerestories, some with windows; each offering a different intensity and color of light—that distinguish his design. And it is from both the reinforcement of the axial plan and the celebration of natural light that our present restoration takes its premise."

Hardy Holzman Pfeiffer's success in St. Louis was rooted as much in the firm's technological sophistication as in its grasp of the subtleties of Gilbert's design. Their first task was to respond to the museum's need for a better physical environment for its art.

By 1973, soon after the restoration and new construction program began, the building's original skylights, then 69 years old, were badly corroded. Rain leaked through them and, as already noted, they admitted far too much daylight for proper conservation of the art. The artificial lighting was entirely inadequate, wall and ceiling surfaces were in bad repair, and the floor surfaces were an ill-assorted collection of materials—marble, soapstone, tile, and wood, which failed to reinforce the geometric order of the Beaux Arts plan. Here and there were doorways and furnishings of today's dimensions, looking dinky and forlorn in the vast rooms. So many ill-proportioned spaces had been installed within Gilbert's halls and rooms that it required today's equivalent of Beaux Arts training to sense the presence of a once vigorously legible order.

As we now see, it was all there: rectangles within rectangles forming the well-articulated network of halls, vestibules and stairs connecting rooms related to each other within a carefully graded hierarchy of volumes. HHP's restoration allows the public once again to be accommodated grandly, invited to make its way on foot up the main staircase and into the Sculpture Hall and on into spaces designed to be experienced as walked through—fine passages forming a succession of axes, cross axes and cross-cross axes.

Although the architects were invited to restore only the galleries to the southeast of the Sculpture Hall, there they have made a consequential gesture toward re-establishing the building's symmetry.

The axes once more accommodate sight as well as movement. On the principal facade a niche was transformed into a window to provide a view down a secondary axis of the building to the surrounding park (photos right). By this adjustment HHP improved Gilbert's building by honoring in one more way the Beaux Arts principle that the composition of the interior be made manifest on the exterior.

For this project, appropriately, the architects did everything possible to conceal the sophisticated new climate control and security systems required to meet the standards of environmental quality for today's museums. All such equipment has been located within the original walls and fan rooms and in a new partially buried concrete structure.

Connoisseurs of HHP's exposed ductwork painted lavender or green must look hard to find a single specimen in the St. Louis restoration. There is an exposed duct in the print gallery—a personal signature. It is lavender and the only one.

THE ST. LOUIS ART MUSEUM, St. Louis, Missouri. Architects: *Hardy Holzman Pfeiffer Associates—partner-in-charge: Hugh Hardy; project architect: Alec W. Gibson.* Consultants: *Peckham & Guyton* (field architects); *LeMessurier Associates/SCI* (structural); *Crawford & White* (mechanical); *Van & Vierse* (electrical); *Jules Fisher & Paul Marantz, Inc.* (lighting). Construction manager: *Howard Needles Tammen & Bergendoff, Inc.* General contractor: *Dickie Construction Co.*

4
AN ART DECO MOVIE HOUSE OF 1931 TRANSFORMED INTO A MULTI-USE THEATER

Once referred to as "Aurora's most precious jewel," this former film palace with a stage for vaudeville was designed by two forgotten masters of the Art Deco style—C.W. and George Rapp. Had not these thirties architects made it possible for the last of the doomed vaudevillians to perform "live" in a theater designed for the wonderful new "talkies," there would have been no stage for today's live instrumentalists, singers, actors and dancers.

The remodeling of the entire building, badly neglected for at least fifteen years, posed difficult problems. In adapting the movie house into a 1,900-seat theater for symphonic performance, various kinds of smaller musical ensembles, dance and Broad-

way shows, it was necessary to enlarge the old stage considerably in width and depth. In addition to building a thrust apron stage, the architects removed the original plaster proscenium and extended the width of the stage opening to a new frame defined by a pair of existing pilasters on either side of the apron (see page 58). They extended the rear of the stage beyond the fly tower and built new dressing rooms on the perimeter and above this extension (section above).

A wide slot for stage lighting was cut into the existing suspended ornamental plaster ceiling of the auditorium (see page 58) and new rigging was added over the thrust stage (section above). The acoustical consultants, Charles Boner Associates, recommended that

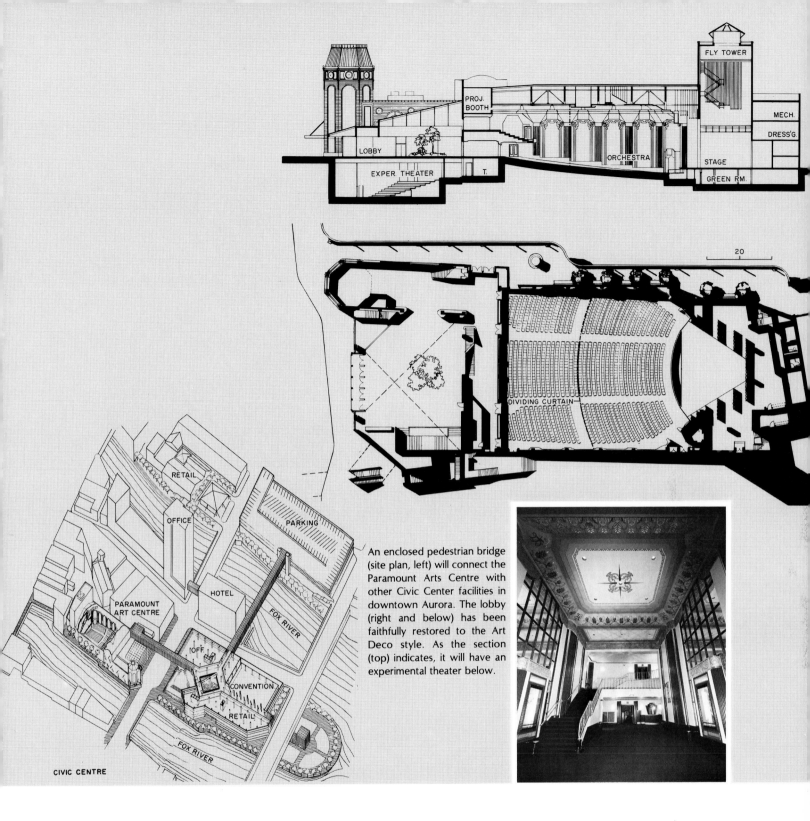

An enclosed pedestrian bridge (site plan, left) will connect the Paramount Arts Centre with other Civic Center facilities in downtown Aurora. The lobby (right and below) has been faithfully restored to the Art Deco style. As the section (top) indicates, it will have an experimental theater below.

hard reflective panels be placed behind the formerly sound absorbent murals between the pilasters. Absorbent panels were placed at the rear wall of the house.

The architects improved the sight lines by altering the floor and balcony profiles. The original movie seating has been restored and realigned for a theater audience with provision for 36 handicapped wheelchair patrons in the center of the main floor of the house. There are no steps for the handicapped to climb on this floor and telephone booths and drinking fountains are low enough to be used by people in wheelchairs. Special washrooms are provided for them and main floor emergency exits are ramped. Parking stalls have been reserved for them and the curb near

the theater entrance is also ramped.

The ornament of the grand lobby and the auditorium has been meticulously restored in the palette of colors and materials of the Art Deco period. The exterior facades have been restored as well. These consist of patterned brick with inset terra cotta panels ornamenting the entrance and the side exits. The brick and terra cotta have been cleaned, repaired and restored. In addition, the marquee and sign have been rebuilt to the original designs. The badly deteriorated River Promenade, parallel to the long axis of the theater, has been rebuilt, cantilevered over the river, landscaped and lighted to tie it into the other streetscape work which is part of the ongoing downtown development.

THE PARAMOUNT ARTS CENTRE, Aurora, Illinois. Owner: *Aurora Civic Center Authority*. Architects: *Elbasani Logan Severin Freeman—partner-in-charge: Geoffrey Freeman; project architect: Peter Aaron; designers: Lynn Ross Malloy, Leon Parham.* Architects for construction supervision only: *Frazier Orr Fairbank Quam.* Consultants: *The Office of Irving Cantor* (structural); *Segner & Dalton* (mechanical/electrical); *Charles Boner Associates* (acoustical); *Ralph Alswang-Theater Planning Associates* (lighting and theater); *Dean Abbott* (landscape); *Harold Miller* (costs). General contractor: *R.C. Wegman Construction Co.*

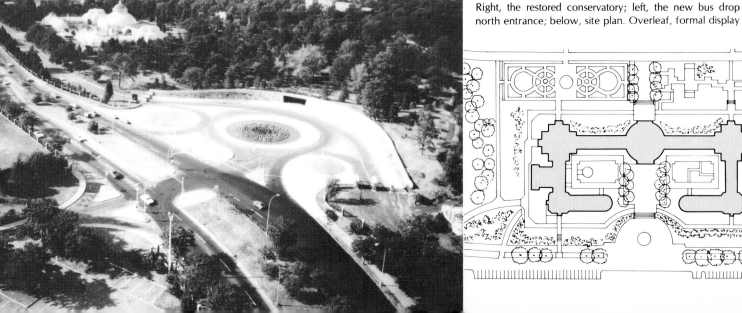

Right, the restored conservatory; left, the new bus drop off; top, the north entrance; below, site plan. Overleaf, formal display house.

5
RESTORING A VICTORIAN BOTANICAL CONSERVATORY

The Conservatory of the New York Botanical Garden must be the most otherworldly place in the Bronx—or anywhere else, for that matter. Set on a formal grassed podium, the turn of the century steel-and-glass structure rises off the lawn in white-boned translucent Beaux-Arts bubbles. At once tropical and Victorian, the low, arched, domed building, full of exotic flora, seems to belong in some Jamesian era of crinolines and bizarre feathered hats. Begun in 1899 and attributed to William R. Cobb, architect for the still-extant greenhouse manufacturers Lord and Burnham, the recently-landmarked Conservatory is a rare and lovely example of a period greenhouse C-shaped in plan. The atmospheric beauty of this cathedral built to nature inspires not only fantasy but awe; the building commands respectful attention, both for itself and for the man-made Eden it shelters from the real Bronx outside.

It's hard to believe, but true, that a little over five years ago the structure was considered a white elephant by the Garden, and was threatened with demolition. After all, administrators argued, the building had been remodeled twice in 1938 and 1953, with results judged disastrous with accelerating rapidity. The '30s restoration, reflecting the drastic change in taste since the beginning of the century, stripped the building of its ornate cresting and simplified its Victorian detail; fifteen years later, the Park Service severely mutilated the building, hacking off two Italian Renaissance vestibules to replace them with a brick wall and WPA-style entry.

So, in the heyday of what New York cultural institutions remember as the Hoving era, and City Hall recalls as the Lindsay epoch—a time of grand plans for cultural facilities—the Garden called in the architectural firm of Edward Larrabee Barnes to do a new master plan with a view to eliminating the Conservatory and constructing a new building on the site. To Barnes's credit, he supported the minority preservationist call to save and renovate the Conservatory. But subsequent changes in policy and funding have meant that while the Conservatory has been restored, the rest of Barnes's plan, including his project for the new Plants and Man building, is on indefinite hold.

Begun in piecemeal fashion on a shoestring city budget, the Conservatory's restoration was completed thanks to a gift from Enid Annenberg Haupt. This funding supported a thorough structural and mechanical rehauling, but did not allow for any "luxuries," esthetic or technical.

The most devastating consequence of the cutback in the master plan was that the restored Conservatory would have to house the educational exhibits originally intended for the Plants and Man building and handle the traffic that these entail. Barnes, who looked forward to restoring the Conservatory to its former leisurely elegance, complete with decorative gar-

dens, is undisguisedly "regretful that this building had to become a large-scale teaching facility."

One particularly disturbing result of the expanded function of the Conservatory is a radical alteration of the circulation scheme. Originally, one approached the conservatory in processional Beaux-Arts style, passing between the enclosing wings, through the courtyard and into the domed central pavilion. From here one strolled through either ell, reversed direction and returned to repeat the promenade on the other side. This radial circulation pattern, however conducive to contemplation of the flora, simply won't work, the Garden realized at the last minute, for large groups. Accordingly, the Garden requested the architects to link the two end greenhouses by a tunnel, creating an efficient circulation loop (see plan page 64) but "severely damaging the architectural experience of the building"—as Barnes has pointed out.

This tunnel, done at rock-bottom cost, is a galvanized steel culvert-type connection curved in an onion shape. Necessary as it is, this crude element forms a jarring contrast with the elegant domes of steel tracery above. So, unfortunately, does a second structural intervention necessitated by the educational program: a large cement stair leading to a basement teaching area below house 1 (plan, page 64).

The damage to the Beaux-Arts axiality and the sequential ordering of the spaces is compounded by the present entrance, into a corner pavilion. Barnes has, however, done a good deal to correct this problem, and to recapture the axes, in reorienting the approaches to the building. One now enters the Garden and approaches the conservatory via a new main entrance (photo, bottom left, page 60). Designed as a bus and auto drop off, the eye-shaped entrance is outlined by a curved wall, an eyebrow of Cyclopean masonry that seems to rise out of the natural rock outcroppings at the right, becoming progressively manmade in appearance. The wall, and the planted berm behind it, are pierced by a pedestrian tunnel; moving through this passage, those approaching on foot lose the roar of the street and emerge in the green garden.

Barnes has also endeavored to re-establish an axial entrance to the Conservatory itself (plan, page 64). When ongoing road work is completed, visitors will approach the building from what was originally the rear, entering on axis on the north side of the central pavilion.

The north side, however, is quite worthy to welcome visitors, being one of the highlights of the exterior renovation (photo, top right page 60). Both the original entrance vestibules to the central greenhouse were essentially demolished in the brutal '58 remodeling; and the original working drawings had been lost. From old photographs and a few original, not very detailed drawings, project architect Siglinde Stern reconstructed the vestibules inside and out. Because of budgetary constraints, the original cast-iron facades of the vestibules had to be rebuilt in cast aluminum, and the decorative paning, both here and in the fan windows, was replaced by sheet glass with metal filigree work superimposed. Although some corners were cut in the final realization (some of the planned filigree was omitted, leaving the larger panes a bit bleak) the effect is nonetheless one of magnificence.

Though the restoration of the vestibules may be the most visible and, from a historical point of view, the most impressive part of the project, the fundamental, meat-and-potatoes work was concerned with the structural and mechanical systems. In a slowly-moving sequential renovation, each piece of the steel was stripped, tested, and, if necessary, replaced. The glass skin underwent a similar process. The existing mullions had replaced the original Victorian mullions in 1938, when the elaborate six-mullioned bays were altered to a simpler module of four mullions. The extant mullions, however, constituted a sophisticated response to the problems posed by the humid interior. Each of the galvanized metal U-sections had cypress inserts, into which the glass was set with putty. (Cypress is one of two woods naturally resistant to damp—the other being the much softer redwood.) Each

A Partition, historical display house

B New stairs to lower level

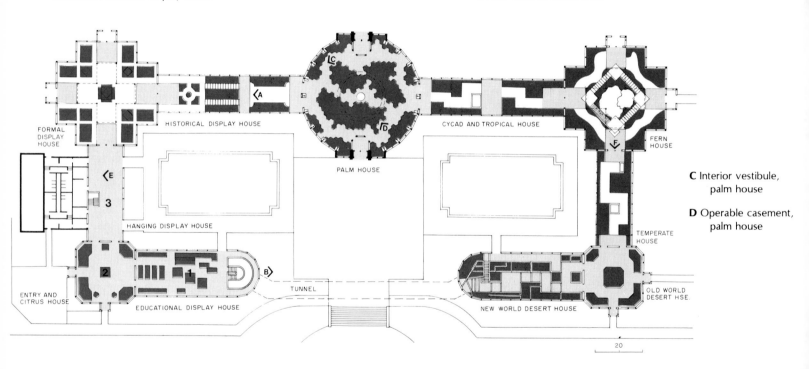

FORMAL
DISPLAY
HOUSE

HISTORICAL DISPLAY HOUSE

PALM HOUSE

CYCAD AND TROPICAL HOUSE

FERN
HOUSE

HANGING DISPLAY HOUSE

TEMPERATE
HOUSE

ENTRY AND
CITRUS HOUSE

EDUCATIONAL DISPLAY HOUSE

TUNNEL

NEW WORLD DESERT HOUSE

OLD WORLD
DESERT HSE.

20

C Interior vestibule,
palm house

D Operable casement,
palm house

F Catwalk, fern house

E Mirror wall, hanging display house

cypress-lined mullion was carefully repaired and re-used: where this was not possible, redwood was substituted. The alternative—to replace the steel-and-wood mullions with modern aluminum ones—"would have made the whole building fat," as Barnes puts it; the thicker bands of soft metal would have destroyed the fine strong lines of the steel frame.

Concentrating on essentials, the architects also modernized heating, wiring, and piping systems. In addition to replacing and repairing roof and side wall ventilators, the architects made several of the large vertical windows operable, creating badly-needed ventilation. In an intervention as simply beautiful as it is ingenious, the architects devised a manually operable wheel- and-gear system to open the huge casements. Reminiscent of early industrial window opening systems and of such famous early modern offspring of these as Le Corbusier's window systems in the Maison de Verre, the hand-operable, visible mechanism is a sophisticated recapturing, on a small scale, of the somewhat naive delight in the machine, and in man's ability to tune the built environment, which the Conservatory itself embodies.

Lastly, a small and relatively spontaneous structural alteration combines efficiency with esthetics. A new boiler house, done just before Barnes came to the job, met the Conservatory with a brick-walled intrusion, enclosing a stair, and sealed off that side of greenhouse 3 (see plan) with a blank wall. Cutting down the stairwell so that its brick edge appears to be another planter, project architect Alistair Bevington also conceived of duplicating, on the partition separating the greenhouse from the offices (also housed within the walls of the boiler structure) the elevation of the glass wall opposite, which gives on to the court. The "fake," realized in mirrored one-way glass, so that those in the offices can see without being seen, visually opens up that side of the greenhouse (photo, bottom center page 64).

Moreover, constructing an "outside" wall on an interior partition is perfectly in the spirit of the original architecture. The varied prisms of the eleven greenhouses that compose the conservatory meet each other with no intermediary concessions; the skin of the domed polygonal volumes continues uninterrupted across the space enclosed by the long vaulted elements. The outside wall, unchanged, becomes interior divider in the middle of a fan window (photo, top left, page 64). This simple additive method of construction, in which one greenhouse is just stuck on to the next, creates serendipitously sophisticated architecture by throwing into high relief the ambiguities of this glass house, inside which man makes the outside of his dreams, a nature tamed, ordered, and made to do tricks. In a greenhouse, inside *is* outside.

Details like the reconstruction of the vestibules, the window systems and the mirror wall exemplify the sensitive spirit of this restoration. The renovation of this spectacular yet terribly delicate landmark called for no grand costly gestures, no daring juxtapositions of new and old, no flamboyant innovation, but rather for a quiet, direct rebuilding of the original. Barnes's office has carried out repairs and renovations with a necessary economy of means which seems to have sparked a small wealth of invention. The restoration preserves the elusive, unquantifiable exhilaration of the architecture, and the shimmering domes retain a younger century's poignant marveling at man's capacity to fashion a machine-house for making a garden in. —*Eleni M. Constantine*

ENID A. HAUPT CONSERVATORY, New York Botanical Garden, Bronx, New York. Architects: *Edward Larrabee Barnes*—associates-in-charge: *Percy Keck, Alistair Bevington;* project architects: *Siglinde Stern, Michael Timchula, Hillary Brown.* Consultants: *Weidlinger Associates* (structural soils); *Arthur Edwards* (mechanical electrical); *David Klepper* (acoustical); *Donald Bliss* (lighting); *Vignelli Associates* (graphics). Landscape architects: *Kiley, Tindall, Walker*—partner in-charge: *Peter Walker.* General contractor: *Louisa Construction Co., Inc.*—superintendent: *Angelo Sisca.*

6
A NEW LANDMARK CENTER FOR ST. PAUL

In 1971 former president Nixon signed an Executive order that directed the General Services Administration to provide leadership in maintaining the historical and cultural environment in the United States. GSA, in other words, was to become a preservationist, and it was asked to begin at home by surveying its more than ten thousand buildings to single out those of special historical and architectural worth, nominating the ones it found to the National Register. Very shortly thereafter, the GSA established its Office of Fine Arts and Historic Preservation, and, most importantly, it drafted and sponsored a Surplus Property Act Amendment (Public Law 92-362), which was passed by the Congress in 1972.

This was the stitch in time for a growing and growingly frustrated band of city officials and private citizens in St. Paul, Minnesota, who had been trying for years finally to implement a plan to put the Old Federal Courts Building back to some good use. The building had been a centerpiece in the architecture of downtown St. Paul, and as downtown had decayed over the years so had the centerpiece, so that when the Federal government moved out in 1965 the Old Federal Courts Building was a sorry shadow of its former self. But if the building's decline had paralleled the decline of the downtown, why should not the reverse also be possible, with a renovation of the building serving as a symbol for the revitalization of a whole area? Besides, it was handsome, and it also contained a great deal of space that could be put to some good use.

The problem was in finding the precise use, finding the money, and—above all—finding the way to meet the government's stringent requirements for transferring the building to local hands. Until 1972, the Surplus Property Act provided that, once a building had been declared surplus, it could either be sold for its appraised price to anyone or it could be given away to some non-profit, non-revenue-producing group whose activities benefited the general public. But a further condition of this latter possibility was that the group in question would also be subject to the detailed approval of either the Department of Health, Education, and Welfare or

Shin Koyama photos

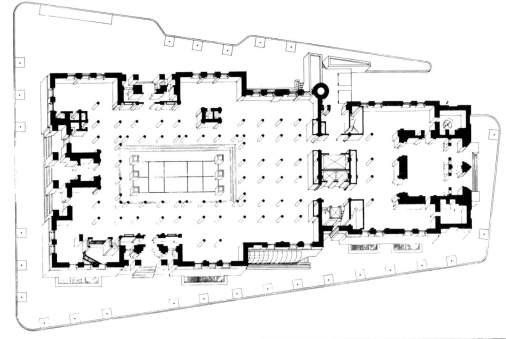

The photograph on the opposite page shows the Fifth Street elevation of the Old Federal Courts Building in St. Paul—now converted into a public cultural center and renamed "Landmark Center." A plan of the main floor of the building is shown on the right.

the Department of the Interior, depending on the nature of its activities. Enthusiasts in St. Paul for the renovation of the Old Federal Courts Building had tried without success to buy the building outright from the Federal government (noting that money paid to purchase it would reduce dangerously the coffers for its renovation), and they had also developed a number of specific proposals for uses that, it was hoped, would qualify the building for being given away outright by the government. All of these had been rejected by the bureaucracies.

The Congress (and the General Services Administration) simplified the entire process in 1972 and provided a much-needed break in the log jam. Now to be eligible for transfer, a Federal building had only to be surplus property, to be on the National Register, and to be the subject of an adequately funded plan for adaptive re-use. It could now be used for revenue-producing purposes and for a broad range of activities, as long as its status as a public historic landmark was not violated.

And so in October, 1972, the Old Federal Courts Building was turned over to the City of St. Paul for the token sum of one dollar. A principal occupant was to be the St. Paul Ramsey Arts and Science Council—a vigorous centralized administrative and fund-raising agency for most of St. Paul's and surrounding Ramsey County's artistic and scientific organizations.

The original building was designed and constructed from 1892 to 1902 by the United States Treasury Department under the architectural direction of Willoughby J. Edbrooke and James Knox Taylor. The first steps in its renovation and restoration—begun in 1973 by St. Paul architect Brooks Cavin—were the cleaning of the warm, pink St. Cloud granite of which the building is built and the replacement of the existing composition roof with one made of clay tiles from the original molds rediscovered in Ohio. At this time three of the original courtrooms were partially restored for public meetings and recitals.

While this was happening, an initial programming study and a preliminary budget were also being prepared by the firm of Dober Associates in Cambridge, Massachusetts. In 1974, the firms of Perry, Dean, Stahl & Rogers, in Boston, and Winsor/Faricy, in St. Paul, were selected to prepare the final re-use scheme. This creates facilities for a new 250-seat auditorium, for shops, restaurants, art galleries, and it provides offices for the Arts and Science Council and its members. It also provides for restoration of not just the original three but four courtrooms, and, perhaps most important of all for the public's perception of the building, the high central court of the building has now been restored. This space, which is shown on the previous page, originally had three ceilings—one at the very top, another two floors below that, and one between the first and second floors to provide security for the post office that used to be there. The lower ceiling has now been removed, giving for the first time the chance for the visitor on the first floor to see this remarkable space in a single glance. In the space directly below the roof at the very top a greenhouse enlivens what was formerly an attic, as the plans on the following pages illustrate. It is surrounded by a museum art school and by additional space still unassigned, waiting for some future occupants.

Though still not yet fully complete, the Old Federal Courts Building has been sufficiently refurbished, sufficiently altered, and sufficiently loved so that it has now become the Landmark Center its supporters and creators wanted it to be. It is worth noting that there are now other similar projects under way because of the 1972 amendment to the Surplus Property Act. But it is also worth noting that there are still other projects—like the renovation of the Old Federal Building in St. Louis or of the Customhouse in New York—which are *not* under way (or if they are, under different sails) because no suitable local takers could be found. Nothing worthwhile happens quite automatically, and so while it seems certainly fair to say that GSA's initiative in the Surplus Property Act was imaginative, so does it have to be said that the citizens of St. Paul deserve due credit for their persistence in realizing its possibilities— as well as, perhaps, in helping to create the environment for it in the first place.

Shin Koyama photos

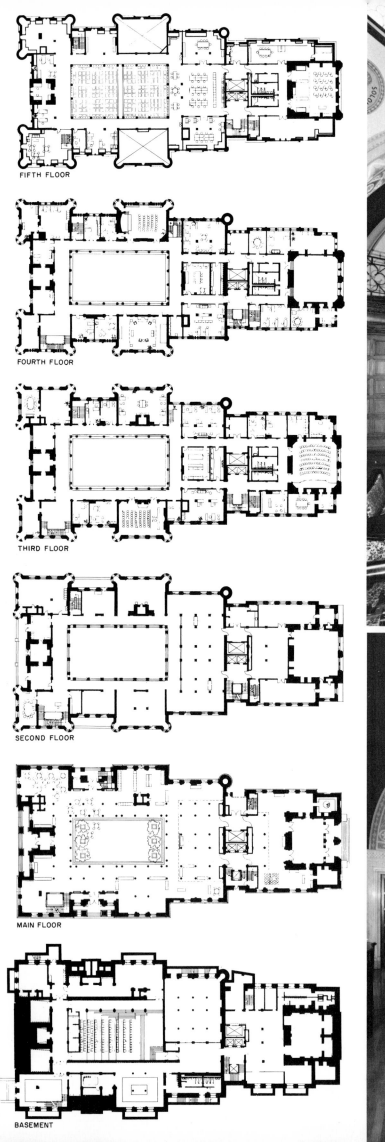

FIFTH FLOOR

FOURTH FLOOR

THIRD FLOOR

SECOND FLOOR

MAIN FLOOR

BASEMENT

The color photograph on the opposite page shows the restored law library in Landmark Center. The lighting was recreated from early photographs, and other details were handled with equal meticulousness in this purely restorational part of the project. Also restored was the Superior Court room shown on the left. The photograph on the right shows the marble foyer under the north tower, and the photographs above show the arcades around the central court inside.

Shin Koyama photos

7
A 19th-CENTURY COURTHOUSE CONSERVED

Balthazar Korab photos

The restoration of the interiors is quite expansive and inclusive, composed of a maze of intricate details that combine for enormous visual impact. Color, form and pattern research led to remaking sculpted spaces like the stairway (above) and the impressive courtroom (right). One treasured detail is the mascaron (below) glistening above a doorway.

The revitalization of the 1889 Livingston County Courthouse in Howell, Michigan, near Detroit, is a preservation success story in which the architects restored the best elements of the original design while consciously creating an esthetically pleasing contrast between the old and the new. The courthouse was in a deplorable state with a leaky roof, fire hazards, and inadequate plumbing, mechanical and electrical systems. Once the city's commissioners realized the need for better working space, a Courthouse Preservation Committee was established to undertake necessary preliminary work to discover whether the courthouse was worth saving. The search for an architect was initiated. Twenty-four architectural firms were invited to submit their qualifications. With the aid of the County Planning Department and the Building Preservation Committee, the field was narrowed to three; after final interviews, William Kessler and Associates was hired, with Chambers and Chambers as restoration consultant.

In preparation of a feasibility study, it was discovered that the original drawings were lost. Instead of laboriously preparing measured drawings, rectified photography— a photographic method that allows negatives of predetermined size to be enlarged to a convenient architectural scale and printed on photo-sensitive drafting film—was used to create base information from which working drawings could be prepared. To augment this, historical records were unearthed, including old minutes recorded by the Board of Commissioners in 1889, construction specifications, postcards and photographs.

Despite the building's disrepair, the architects found it to be structurally sound. "The masonry walls were still strong, requiring only pointing to protect their integrity, and the wood floor joists were more than adequate for office loading," states architect Edward Francis, principal-in-charge. The feasibility study enumerated the social as well as the practical reasons for preservation—but emphasized the lower cost and reduced time for rehabilitation.

Financing became a dilemma. How does a small town raise the necessary funds for saving such a structure? "We rejected the traditional bake sale as a fund-raising method," declares Lynne Jamieson, a commissioner at the time, chair of Courthouse Preservation Committee, and prime crusader throughout the process. After the Board voted "in favor of practicality [of rehabilitation], referendum petitions appeared. Rumors abounded. Charges and countercharges were made. Recall was in the air. Every ill of county government was blamed on the courthouse . . . It became one of the biggest political battles in the County's history," continues Jamieson. "Friends of the Livingston County Courthouse" was created—a small but dedicated army that lobbied for passage of a bond issue to finance courthouse work. The majority of the final cost of $1.5 million came from the passage of this

bond issue, supplemented by grants from the Michigan History Division, a department of the Secretary of State's office.

The scope of the work is quite diverse, with partial restoration and partial rehabilitation. While the exterior was restored, the prime focus was on the interiors. The courtroom had suffered greatly from past ''modernization'' attempts. The original coffered ceiling was discovered after the removal of a suspended acoustical ceiling. And to the surprise of workers, original and elaborate frescoes were exposed underneath four layers of paint. Furnishings—desks, chairs, shelving, hardware and wickets—and plaster wainscoting, called ''adamant,'' were also intact. Because of the fresco work and acoustical considerations, there was an unusual approach to the new ceiling: the architects designed a vinyl-covered acoustical panel, suspended in the coffers, colored to match the background of the frescoes, onto which artist Darla Olson recreated the fresco design on the acoustical panel without affecting its sound-absorption qualities.

The restoration of the frescoes was accomplished by a small team of CETA employees under the direction of Darla Olson. Each of the painted patterns of the restored artwork was documented with a color photograph, tracing and rough sketch with dimensional notations and color hues.

Improvements also included the rearrangement of spaces on all floors to provide convenient work areas and better circulation for barrier-free and fire safety regulations; new plumbing, mechanical and electrical systems; addition of judge's reception area with special access to court and adjacent rooms; and a hydraulic elevator with a rear door for delivery of prisoners without crossing public areas. Most importantly, a mezzanine was inserted above but open to the formerly unused attic. Construction of a skylight on the inside faces of two existing roof pyramids permitted daylight into this space and unusual views to the clock tower.

''The opportunity exists to maintain notable structures that humanize the townscape and serve to reinforce the rural tradition of the county,'' argues the architect. ''The courthouse, restored to its earlier grandeur, stands as an impressive symbol of what can be accomplished when a community's citizens work together. It proudly demonstrates that the best from our past can retain validity and impact for generations.''

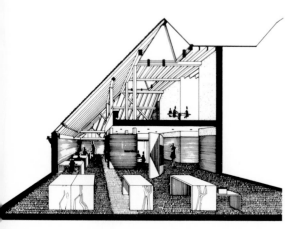

The mezzanine as the newest space was inserted above the attic level, providing a partially enclosed employee lounge (above and below), with daylight from a skylight.

LIVINGSTON COUNTY COURTHOUSE, Howell, Michigan. Owner: *Livingston County Board of Commissioners—Commissioner Lynne Jamieson, owner's representative.* Architects: *William Kessler and Associates—Edward D. Francis, FAIA, principal-in-charge.* Engineers: *McClurg and Associates, Inc.* (structural); *Hoyem-Basso Associates, Inc.* (mechanical/electrical). Consultants: *Chambers and Chambers* (restoration architect); *Klepper, Marshall, King Associates, Ltd.* (acoustical); *Darla Olson* (artist and director of art restoration). General contractor: *Elgin Builders, Inc.*

MEZZANINE FLOOR

ATTIC FLOOR

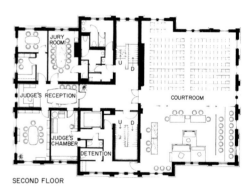

SECOND FLOOR

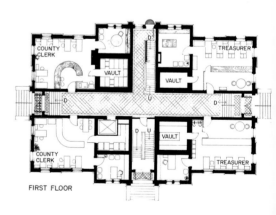

FIRST FLOOR

GROUND FLOOR

The brilliancy of the original exterior detailing is a splendid example of Richardsonian Romanesque, the style adapted by the original architect, Albert E. French, for the Livingston County courthouse. Outstanding characteristics include round arches and massive articulated walls, here with rugged, rough-cut native stone in earthy colors. A large arch at the entrance, with a carved capital (middle, below), sets the stage for repetitious arched fenestration, underneath which is multi-patterned ornament (below). Above the arched windows on the lower level is a corbelled brick molding (bottom).

1 Lobby
2 Orangerie
3 **Aztec Lounge**
4 Ballroom
5 Conference Center 1979
6 Cottages
7 Valley Wing 1979
8 Paradise Wing 1975
9 Pool
10 Foyer

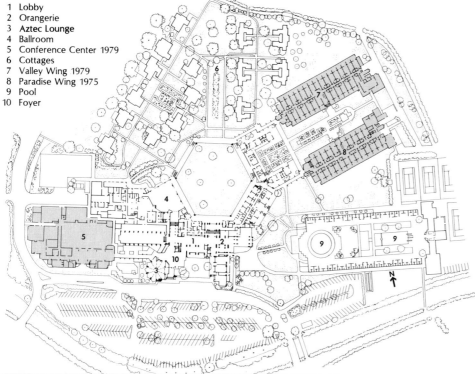

8
RESTORING AND EXTENDING THE ARIZONA BILTMORE

The 1929 June issue of ARCHITECTURAL RECORD credits Albert Chase McArthur as the architect for the Arizona Biltmore Hotel. But it comes as little surprise to discover that McArthur worked as a draftsman in the Oak Park Studio of Frank Lloyd Wright. When McArthur's two brothers conceived the idea for an elegant resort hotel, they naturally handed the job to their brother, and he in turn naturally requested the assistance of his former mentor. Though Wright must have balked at anything less than top billing, a resort complex in the midst of the Arizona desert would have been an irresistable opportunity to display his theory of "Organic Architecture." And, according to Olgivanna Lloyd Wright, "To spare the destruction of the landscape had in fact been my husband's lifelong thesis in relation to what is now termed environmental planning."

Wright's theories about an architecture synchronized with the landscape could have found no better proving ground than the Arizona Biltmore; the hotel rises discreetly from an arid mesa, and is composed of forms and materials that are clearly derived from the

desert terrain and the indigenous flora. In keeping with the spirit and texture of the desertscape, Wright used the humble concrete block as the primary interior and exterior building material. At the time, concrete block was considered the "vulgarian" of the construction industry, but Wright was determined to raise the lowly block to esthetic respectability. The blocks were all molded on site with exquisite details and patterns designed by McArthur and Wright.

The Biltmore opened in February of 1929, and crowned "Jewel of the Desert." Only a few months later the stock market crash brought the Depression and the hotel was purchased by chewing gum magnate William Wrigley, along with 1200 acres of adjacent land. Wrigley saw his role not only as owner, but benefactor—each year the hotel's operating deficit was paid off by a personal check.

Since the halcyon days of Wrigley and the leisure class, the Arizona Biltmore has undergone some dramatic alterations. But with the guidance of John Rattenbury of Taliesin West, Wright's only existing hotel retains its original splendor.

The main building materials for the hotel—copper for the roof, gold for the ceiling, and sand for the concrete block—are all indigenous to Arizona. The Aztec Lounge (right) with its sharply attenuated roof (top) is adjacent to the hotel entrance. The main lobby (below) is reached after first passing through a foyer that contains a symbolic oasis and a 1927 mural by Wright (right). The mural is the architect's abstraction of the desert flora—using the T-square, triangle, and compass to achieve the design. The lighting system is integrated into the structure, as glass intermittently replaces concrete block.

Markow Photography

Neil Koppes

In June of 1973, the Wrigley family sold the Biltmore to Talley Industries; three weeks later, while workmen were updating the sprinkler system, a welder's torch ignited insulation material and a six-alarm fire completely destroyed the fourth floor of the hotel and gutted the interiors. The new owners were determined to reopen September 29, for the winter season, and a feverish reconstruction effort began.

After interviewing several firms, the new owners commissioned Taliesin Associated Architects of the Frank Lloyd Wright Foundation to oversee the construction. To ensure the authenticity of the project, the architects rallied to the cause with Wright's original drawings on linen from the Foundation's vaults. Concrete block was molded on-site using Arizona sand, duplicating the texture and patterns of the original (the 1929 alumi-

num molds were fortunately saved by the owners and fiberglass form liners were fabricated using the original aluminum molds as matrices). New carpets based on six of Wright's geometric patterns from the early 1920s were woven in Ireland, and two workmen from the 1929 construction job were called out of retirement to teach 15 young workers how to apply the more than 38,000-square-feet of gold leaf onto the "largest gold leaf ceiling in the world."

The copper roof posed an especially tricky problem: how to reproduce the patina created by 44 years of Arizona sun. In what must be the surest testimony of the new owner's commitment to the project, Talley Industries' research staff invented a chemical process to produce the desired patina. And after a miraculous 91 days, the hotel was again open for business.

Many of the designs used in the reconstruction were not from the original Biltmore project: the pattern for the lobby carpet was borrowed from the Imperial Hotel in Tokyo, and some of the furniture was designed by Wright in the 1950s. But it is all *bona fide* Wright—re-interpreted, re-colored, and re-applied for the Biltmore. Ironically, the hotel is more *Wrightian* after reconstruction, and the shared credits seem now to favor Wright over McArthur—even if posthumously.

In 1977, a Canadian investment group purchased the hotel, and with the new owners came a major expansion program. A 120-room addition, the Valley Wing, was built parallel to the 90-room Paradise Wing addition, dating from 1975 (photo top, next page). The two new guest wings have been pushed to the side, behind the original structure, and, as designed by the Taliesin archi-

Balthazar Korab

One of the new guest room additions (above) is joined to the original hotel by a covered walkway (top right). The Orangerie cafe/cabaret (below), with its stalactite chandeliers, flanks the main lobby and was added after the 1973 fire to replace a cocktail lounge. The large photo on the right makes evident the architects' painstaking attention to texture, form, and detail. The concrete block, facing the flue of the fireplace, is perforated with glass inserts to expose flames shooting up the chimney. The furniture is casual, overstuffed, almost domestic, and makes a soothing counterpart to the intricate patterns molded into the concrete block. The carpets are patterned after six of Wright's geometric designs.

Balthazar Korab   Neil Koppes

Markow Photography

tects, are carefully deferential to the original buildings. Although the additions take their inspiration and materials from Wright, they seem less integrated into the landscape and less shaped by the terrain; instead, they provide a sympathetic backdrop.

Nowhere is the hand of Wright more evident than in the hotel interiors—especially the public spaces. A low concrete portico connects the driveway to a foyer that welcomes guests with a symbolic mini-oasis—a freestanding cluster of columns, plants and a waterfall.

Adjacent to the foyer, the circular Aztec Lounge creates the contextural drama for which Wright is famous. As light filters through the glass-filled perforations in the concrete block of the soffit onto the gold ceiling, the room takes on a spectacular aura.

The foyer opens onto a 260-foot-long lobby that serves as the major circulation route for the hotel, leading into restaurants, gardens, and, on each side of the registration desk, to the guest rooms. But the lobby is also one of the more active social areas for the hotel; the scale of the elongated rectangle has been reduced by a mezzanine and small groupings of overstuffed furniture (designed by Wright in the 1950s for Heritage-Henredon, though never manufactured). The lighting system is carefully integrated into the structure, punctuating the columns with opal glass panels shielding metal fixtures on the same module as the concrete block.

All of the guest rooms have been completely refurbished, and each contains a triptych silkscreen adaptation of a Wright mural.

In the fall of last year, a 39,000-square-foot convention center was completed. The Taliesin architects again have designed a low-profile structure that is clearly patterned after the pre-existing buildings.

Since the 1973 fire, $25-million has been spent to expand, maintain, and improve the Arizona Biltmore. In every detail from menu design to staff uniforms, the hotel has received an unparalleled level of attention. The Biltmore remains a brilliant example of "Organic Architecture"—indigenous materials, molded by the landscape, and integrated into a unified complementary whole.

ARIZONA BILTMORE HOTEL, Phoenix, Arizona. Owner: *Rostland Inc.* Architect: *Frank Lloyd Wright Foundation—project architect, John Rattenbury.* Engineers: *Magadini-Alagia Associates (structural); Sergent Hauskins & Beckwith (foundation); Sullivan & Masson (mechanical/electrical).* Consultants: *Frank Lloyd Wright Foundation (interiors/landscape/graphics).* Contractor: *Kitchell Inc.*

3

As American colleges mature, and their buildings age, some become decrepit to the point of being unsafe. Certain collegiate functions disappear — a chapel or a student inn is no longer used. At the same time, more and more colleges and universities do not wish to sacrifice buildings of charm, or sentiment, or structural soundness. The six buildings in this chapter represent similar though distinct solutions, what might be called neo-Eclecticism, an uninhibited combination of period buildings with modern architecture.

Case Western Reserve University, for example, could not bring itself to demolish two sound old buildings, handsome, but no landmarks. Case's architect, Don Hisaka, remodeled them and inserted an atrium and bookstore in between, thus combining all three structures into an up-to-date student center.

Mount Holyoke decided to save what was left of an abandoned inn to preserve the beauty of the row of similar small structures which together made a beautiful New England street. Largely rebuilt, the wood frame building has become one of the college's business and administrative offices.

Syracuse University's Hall of Languages is over 100 years old and was the first building constructed on the campus. More than a sentimental object because of the importance of its site, the awesome grey

CAMPUS BUILDINGS

pile dominates the university from the top of a hill—the centerpiece of a stately row of immense 19th-century academic halls. Deathless stone without, but aging wood within, it posed a challenge to the university. To replace it with a modern building inserted among its sober and majestic neighbors would have been unthinkable. The decision was made, therefore, to completely rebuild the interior while leaving the exterior stone shell intact.

Yale University has always used the leading architects of the day to build its buildings — Russell Sturgis, Bruce Price, James Gamble Rogers, Eero Saarinen, Philip Johnson, and Louis Kahn. In the past decade the school has begun to remodel some of its older buildings, lavishing upon them the care which they deserve. Among the recycled Yale buildings shown in this chapter are an abandoned chapel, the residential halls on the Old Campus, and the Law School.

It is likely that this recycling process will continue to take precedence over new campus construction at Yale and the other older schools included in this chapter. The six examples shown, among the best adaptive work of the past five years, prove that resourceful and inventive architects and their campus clients can find no end of ways to extend the lives of buildings which they venerate.

Photos © Thom Abel except as noted

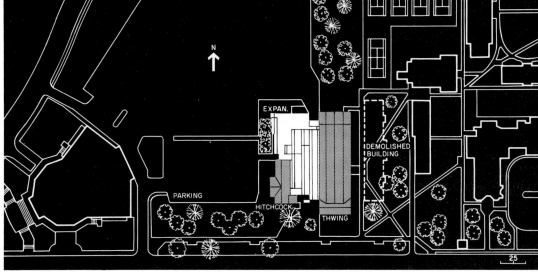

Case Western Reserve Photo Lab

1

CASE WESTERN RESERVE MARRIES OLD BUILDINGS IN NEW STUDENT CENTER

Whatever you call it—modern, post-modern, high tech, or off-the-shelf—Don Hisaka's new in-fill building for Case Western Reserve University's student center behaves with uncommon gallantry. Without compromising its 1980 self, it creates for two older buildings an architectural integrity that did not exist before.

The older and smaller of the two buildings is Hitchcock Hall, at the left of the new structure; it was built in 1897 as a private residence. Thwing Hall, at the right, was built in 1913 as a men's club and saw service as Western Reserve's student activities center even before that university and the Case Institute of Technology, just across Euclid Avenue, merged in 1967.

Beyond their location facing Euclid Avenue and a vaguely Jacobean-Georgian-Eclectic style, the two existing buildings had little in common, least of all in the scales of either their massing or their ornament. Hisaka has boldly inserted between them an L-shaped addition of decided contemporary character. The addition houses a two-story atrium at the front for student milling and lounging and a split-level bookstore at the back.

On the street facade, the designer recessed the in-fill to allow the older buildings apparent precedence along the sidewalk. The

strong horizontals of the new metal window frames and butt glazing align with horizontal elements on each side and thus resolve—or at least blur—discrepancies in scale. At the same time, the horizontals echo the white quoins and stone courses on Thwing and the white lintels above Hitchcock's windows.

Still more, the stepped-back angular peaks of the atrium's monitors establish a sympathetic rhythm in combination with the gables and the front corbiesteps of Hitchcock, while the three planes of the facade repeat the number of arches at Thwing's base. And yet further gallantries to the older buildings include reflections of their exterior detail on the new facade and the re-use of Thwing's old Doric portico, swung 90 degrees from one wall and set at the entrance as a detached portal.

The new front assertively holds its own, nonetheless, both by the emphatic contrast of its light frame and reflective glass with the heavy brick masonry on either side and by its strong composition. Hisaka disposed lights of both reflective and clear glass geometrically to extend the line of the monitors to the base of the addition and to allow glimpses into the lighted atrium even during the day.

The bookstore wing, its facade visible from the parking lot, repeats the general

Milan Bender

composition of the street facade: a glass skin framed by brick masonry. The proportions differ considerably, however, the flat glass structure assuming a far greater importance than it is permitted in front. And although Hitchcock flanks the atrium wall on the right, the stepped masonry on the left is new.

Some architectural pruning was performed on the site as well. Demolition of some earlier additions at the back of Hitchcock was paramount to the form of the new building as it cleared space for the bookstore. Almost equally important was the removal of an extremely undistinguished middle-aged building to the right. Its disappearance opened a grassy vista from Euclid Avenue to part of the campus (see site plan, preceding page). Thwing Center thus gains room enough to stand as a defined entity, its nearest neighbor to old Thwing a rather handsome building of similar design, its neighbor on the Hitchcock side Severance Hall, home of the Cleveland Orchestra.

The same pluralistic approach prevails on the interior of Thwing Center as on the exterior: saving what is beautiful or useful of the old, and straightforwardly revealing the newness of the new—while the architect makes sure that their meetings are affable. In this case, the use of the existing masonry

walls and their glazed windows (the fire department insisted) goes far to establish the easy companionship of old and new. Budget as much as architectural philosophy fostered the pluralism: the 70,000-square-foot building and its furniture cost $3.5 million.

Besides providing circulation for the bookstore and the cafeteria, the atrium sets itself up as a center for casual and deliberate encounters—the bright blue information desk is an easily located and immediately identifiable meeting place. Lounging spaces around the perimeter, such as a platform looking into the bookstore or the preserved front porch of Hitchcock, give semipublic vantage points for watching the passing parade.

Hisaka attributes much of the atrium's vitality to the vision and spirit of CWRU's President Emeritus Louis A. Toepfer, head of the school while Thwing Center was under construction and a man who "understands today's students." It was he who conceived the multicolored neon monogram that clearly identifies the building from the outside and that places the interior squarely within the disco generation.

Because Thwing is so much the larger of the two existing buildings, it accommodates the facilities that can be expected to draw the heaviest traffic. The new cafeteria pluralisti-

The atrium at Case Western Reserve's new student center engages the walls of two different existing buildings as parts of its own interior. Students have direct access to either building—the smaller Hitchcock with new student lounges, or Thwing, with new cafeteria and offices—and to the new split-level bookstore at the rear (right).

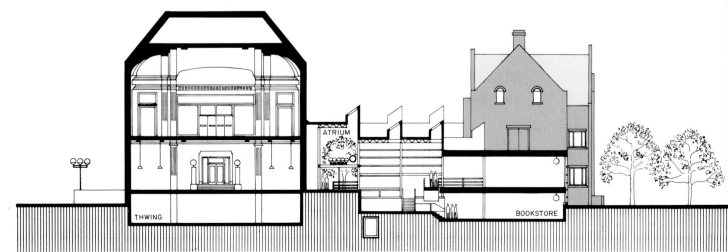

cally mixes new and old design. The imposing fluted columns with their unconventional egg-and-dart capitals were saved, though newly painted; ivory and beige succeeded a color Hisaka describes as "garish yellow." Windows giving onto the central atrium were extended down to the floor, but their carved jambs and lintels and the fluted pilasters, dating from the room's men's-club days, were preserved. Declaring the room's modernity, on the other hand, a row of ceiling lights points straight to food service, accessible beneath the neon-lighted arch that is visually doubled by the mirrored lunette.

Above the unimaginative dropped ceiling in Thwing's second-floor ballroom, Hisaka was overjoyed to discover an elaborately plastered cove ceiling and six oeils-de-boeuf. New decoration is simple: pale violet painted accents, deep magenta draperies, deeper purple stage curtains.

The architect left one room in Thwing unchanged: the art gallery at the front of the building, which boasts a pair of splendidly carved wood chimney breasts. Smaller rooms, newly furnished, house offices for the staff and for student publications, such as two newspapers and the yearbook.

The character of Hitchcock's interior differs yet again. Fittingly enough, the scale of the rooms is domestic, and the building houses intimate lounges and small meeting rooms. The architect has given the main lounge, entered directly from the atrium by the preserved front porch and front door, a dash of glamor by removing the floor above and allowing the room to expand upward. Holes punched in second-floor partitions open views into the room from upstairs and allow the lower room to borrow some light from the atrium via second-floor windows.

The ornament in both old buildings—heavy and masculine in Thwing, dainty and homelike in Hitchcock—is more than handsome, and is virtually irreplaceable today. Metal railings, woodwork, tiles and plaster have been lovingly cleaned, painted and repaired, kept in existence and in use.

THWING CENTER, Case Western Reserve University, Cleveland, Ohio. Architects: *Don M. Hisaka & Associates—Don M. Hisaka, principal-in-charge—design; George Saire, principal; Alex R. Posze, Jr., project architect; Robert Polcar, job captain.* Engineers: *Gensert Bretnall Bobel* (structural); *Pasiadis-Kuentz and Associates* (mechanical); *Mehnert and Frederick* (electrical); *David V. Lewin Corp.* (soils). Interiors: *Don M. Hisaka & Associates.* Construction manager: *J. B. deHamel, Jr. & Associates.* General contractor: *Sam W. Emerson Company.*

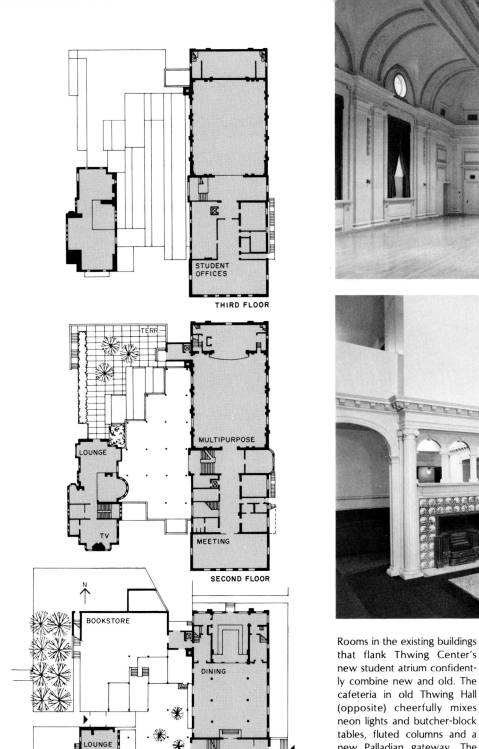

THIRD FLOOR

SECOND FLOOR

FIRST FLOOR
20

Rooms in the existing buildings that flank Thwing Center's new student atrium confidently combine new and old. The cafeteria in old Thwing Hall (opposite) cheerfully mixes neon lights and butcher-block tables, fluted columns and a new Palladian gateway. The ballroom in the same building (at top above) needed only new paint and curtains after its dropped ceiling was removed. In Hitchcock Hall, the main lounge (directly above) expands upward to the attic. Its low cornice molding was retained, however, as were its mantelpiece and the blue tiles that surround the fireplace.

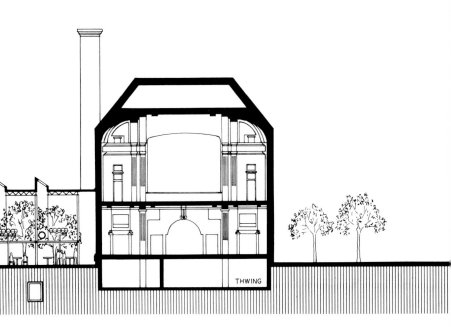

Edward Jacoby/APG photos

2
MOUNT HOLYOKE MIXES YANKEE TRADITION AND THE 20th CENTURY

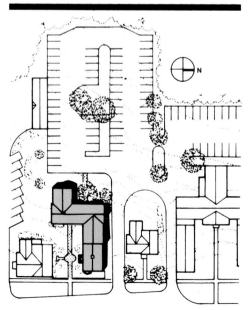

When describing Mount Holyoke's new Newhall Center, architect Elizabeth Ericson draws on the analogy of Grandfather's ax, a transcendent sample of Yankee wit, thrift, ingenuity and respect for tradition: "No matter that it's had eight new handles and two new blades—it's still Grandfather's ax."

Although Mount Holyoke itself occupies large stone collegiate buildings, the campus faces a row of pleasant 19th-century houses of no especial distinction across a street that reflects South Hadley's small-town New England character. The college had put the house that now contains Newhall Center to many uses over the years, most recently as the Bookshop Inn. In search of quarters for its admissions and financial aid offices, the college decided to move into the abandoned inn and to save what could be saved.

That wasn't much, the architect reports—fireplaces, a few timbers, the stone foundation, a stair railing. At the same time, the college wanted the building to look as it did, partly to protect its own view of the New England street, partly as a public relations image for prospective students.

Ericson, a Mount Holyoke alumna and now a principal in Perry, Dean, Stahl & Rogers, prefers to call the building "redesigned," its proportions intact but its period ornament fitting the purse of an owner more affluent than the original. Thus Grandfather's ax.

In addition, however, the existing building had a series of added kitchens and sheds that no one wanted to save. These were demolished and replaced with a new ell forthrightly contemporary in design, particularly on the back elevation, which most visitors will approach from the parking lot. The face of this wing carries a row of obviously contemporary metal-framed windows, and its flush board skin is painted tan to differentiate it still further from white clapboard walls. A steel beam, whose span clearly exceeds anything obtainable from modest balloon-frame structure, supports office space above the void of the entrance portico, but off-the-shelf wood Doric columns recall tradition.

Construction was completed in eight months and cost $518,000.

HARRIET NEWHALL CENTER, Mount Holyoke College, South Hadley, Massachusetts. Architects: *Ericson Associates—Elizabeth Ericson, principal; Donald Corner, job captain; Charles Alexander, Ann Abernathy, team.* Engineers: *Simpson, Gumpertz & Heger* (structural); *BR&A Consulting Engineers* (mechanical/electrical). Landscape architects: *Shurcliffe & Merrill.* Consultant: *Harry Gulesian & Associates* (Colonial design). Contractor: *Fontaine Bros.*

Mount Holyoke's Newhall Center, housing admissions and financial aid offices, presents a traditional Connecticut River Valley residential facade to College Street (top left), its yard a dainty Colonial garden with a picket fence. Via a brick ramp at the rear, which becomes the main facade from the parking lot, visitors approach the central entrance portico with its up-to-date expansive glazing. The Colonial portion of the rear elevation, on the other hand, duplicates the front elevation, sans doorway (top right). The portico, beyond offering a hospitable entrance for prospective students and their parents, provides a visual axis to the campus proper on the other side of College Street. It also provides a meeting place for upper classwomen shepherding new students in the college's Blue Key program. The interiors have a deliberately domestic scale, both because the staff is small in number and to make applicants feel at home. The eclectic furnishings mix spare Yankee furniture, Oriental rugs and modern steel desks. Second-floor space bridging the portico houses clerical staff and record storage shared by the admissions and financial aid departments.

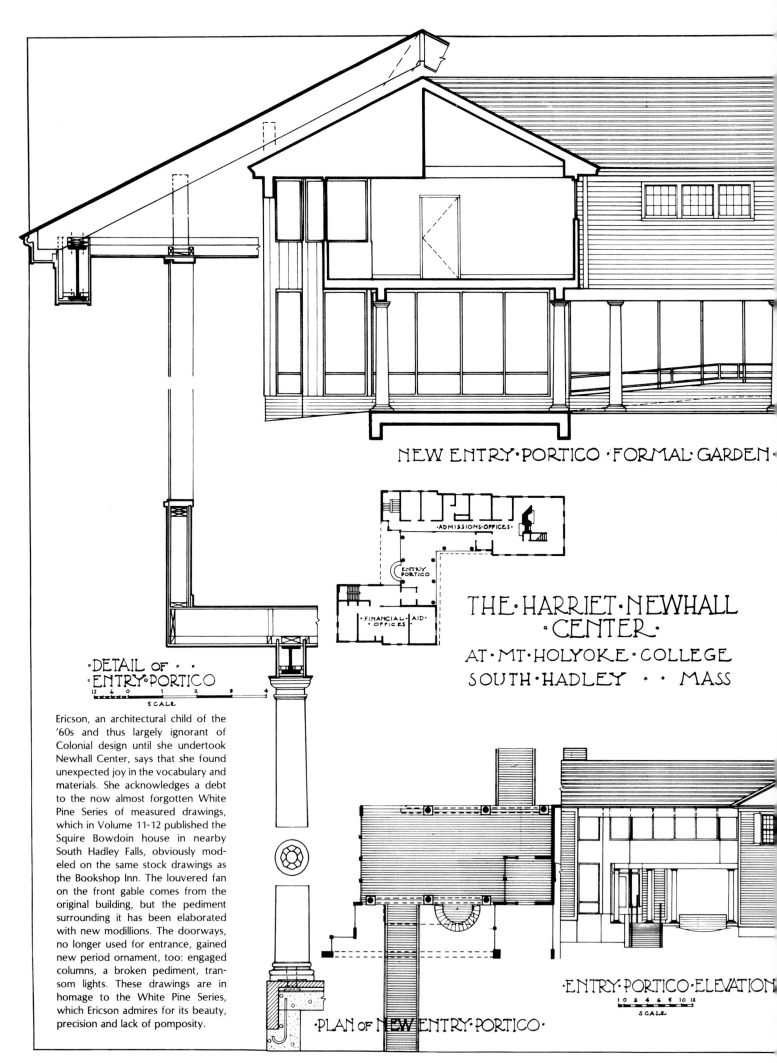

NEW·ENTRY·PORTICO·FORMAL·GARDEN·

·ADMISSIONS·OFFICES·

·ENTRY·PORTICO·

·FINANCIAL· ·AID·
·OFFICES·

THE·HARRIET·NEWHALL
·CENTER·
AT·MT·HOLYOKE·COLLEGE
SOUTH·HADLEY · · MASS

·DETAIL·OF· ·
·ENTRY·PORTICO·
12 6 0   1   2   3   4
SCALE

Ericson, an architectural child of the '60s and thus largely ignorant of Colonial design until she undertook Newhall Center, says that she found unexpected joy in the vocabulary and materials. She acknowledges a debt to the now almost forgotten White Pine Series of measured drawings, which in Volume 11-12 published the Squire Bowdoin house in nearby South Hadley Falls, obviously modeled on the same stock drawings as the Bookshop Inn. The louvered fan on the front gable comes from the original building, but the pediment surrounding it has been elaborated with new modillions. The doorways, no longer used for entrance, gained new period ornament, too: engaged columns, a broken pediment, transom lights. These drawings are in homage to the White Pine Series, which Ericson admires for its beauty, precision and lack of pomposity.

·PLAN·OF·NEW·ENTRY·PORTICO·

·ENTRY·PORTICO·ELEVATION·
1 0 2 4 6 8 10 12
SCALE

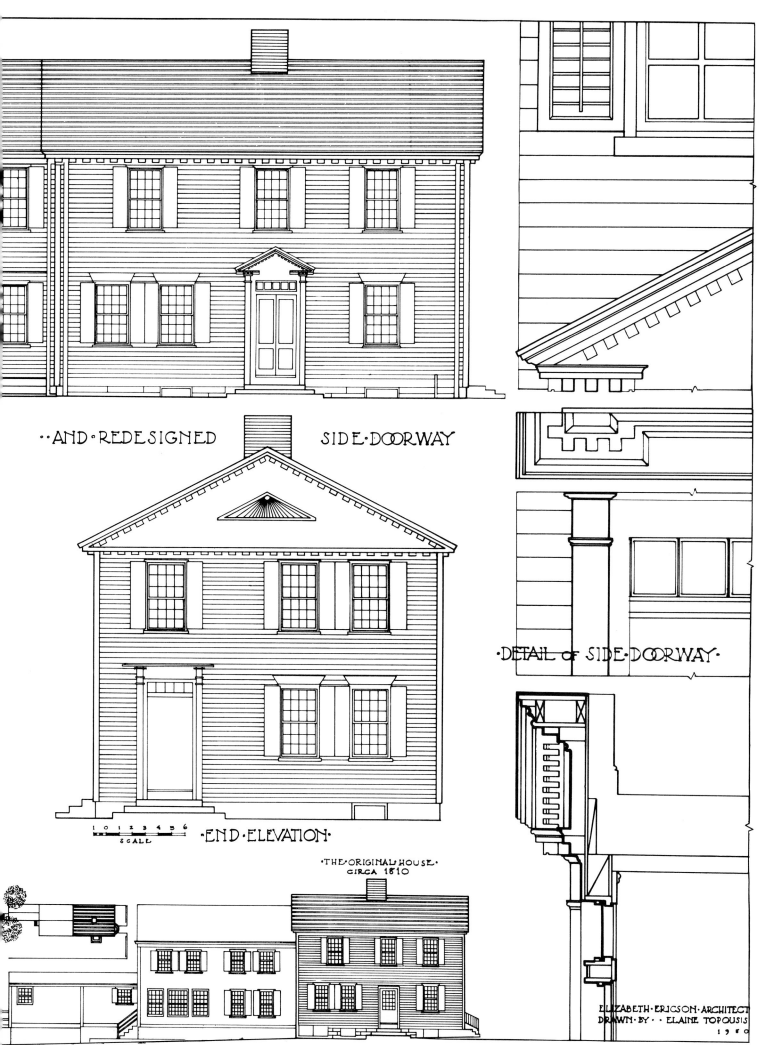

··AND·REDESIGNED   SIDE·DOORWAY

·DETAIL of SIDE·DOORWAY·

·END·ELEVATION·

·THE·ORIGINAL·HOUSE·
CIRCA 1810

ELIZABETH·ERICSON·ARCHITECT
DRAWN·BY··ELAINE·TOPOUSIS
1950

Photos © Steve Rosenthal

3

A MODERN ATRIUM FITS IN A VICTORIAN SHELL AT SYRACUSE UNIVERSITY

For a decade and a half after its opening in 1873, the Hall of Languages *was* Syracuse University, and for more than a hundred years it has served as the center of the school's College of Arts and Sciences.

More than antiquarian sentimentality prompted its salvation from decrepitude and demolition, however. Designed by architect Horatio Nelson White shortly after the Civil War, the Second-Empire-style building sits on the brow of one of Syracuse's seven hills, dominating the area from the top of the long axis of University Avenue and clearly marking the gateway to the campus. Moreover, other late 19th-century buildings flank the Hall of Languages, stretching out on either side to form an imposing architectural collection at the front edge of the campus. The interposition of a modern building in the middle of this row would be, at the least, unseemly.

The architects—Architectural Resources Cambridge for design, Sargent-Webster-Crenshaw & Folley for construction documents and supervision—made very few alterations to the building's exterior. The most visible are the glazed vestibules at the back of the building, through which many of the students enter from the rest of the campus. The enclosed vestibules replace decaying wood porches contemporary with the origi-

nal building. The original "pecked finish" Onondaga limestone bearing walls become the vestibules' interior walls. In addition, the lowering of the floor to grade for the admission of the handicapped to elevators revealed the building's stone foundation.

Apart from the new vestibules, little was altered on the building's exterior. Metal-framed casement sash with thermal glazing replaces the old wood-framed double-hung sash, but the new mullions and muntins repeat the proportions of the old. And cleaning was minimal: one of the architects, Arthur C. Friedel, has a fondness for the "enhancing effect of soil" on ornate stone carving.

But if the exterior of the Hall of Languages remains its old nostalgic self, the same can hardly be said of the interior, now utterly transformed. By all accounts, architect White concentrated his art on the impressive exterior and left the interior to penny-pinching afterthought: vertical T&G board walls, pressed tin ceilings, noisy radiators and a central wood stairway repeatedly described as "quaint"—all still in use in 1978.

The new central stairway sweeps upward through a sloping, five-story atrium. A visitor first opening the Victorian front doors sees a totally unexpected ascent of receding gray and white plaster railings, graduating

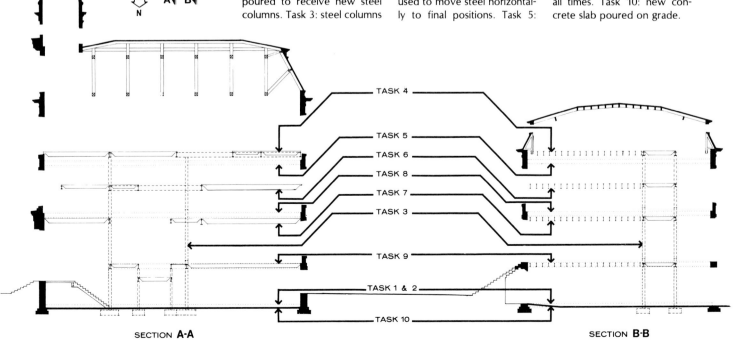

At Syracuse University's Hall of Languages, the replacement of all timber flooring and members except in the mansard roof and the insertion of an extra floor required a phased upside-down gutting procedure: Tasks 1 and 2: existing wood floor removed; footings poured to receive new steel columns. Task 3: steel columns erected through existing wood floors; columns spliced above existing construction, braced by existing floors or new steel members. Task 4: new fifth floor steel framing erected above existing fourth floor; members erected through windows, and existing floor used to move steel horizontally to final positions. Task 5: existing fourth floor removed. Task 6: new fourth floor steel erected. Task 7: new third floor steel erected. Task 8: existing third floor removed. Task 9: removal of existing second floor and erection of new steel phased to provide lateral bracing of stone walls at all times. Task 10: new concrete slab poured on grade.

A◀ B◀

A◀ B◀

N

TASK 4

TASK 5

TASK 6

TASK 8

TASK 7

TASK 3

TASK 9

TASK 1 & 2

TASK 10

SECTION **A-A**

SECTION **B-B**

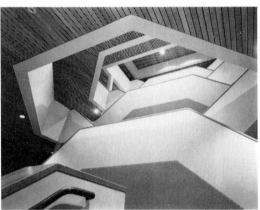

from pale to paler to exaggerate the atrium's apparent height. The first-time user easily comprehends the circulation pattern, however, and despite the geometric monumentality, the scale of the spaces is in fact quite comfortable, almost domestic. The wide corridors around the stairway, paved with bluestone, answer the school's request for generous milling space for students.

The plan places the bulk of heavy student traffic on the lower two floors, although some seminar spaces are located on upper floors. Faculty members have their offices on the top two floors, while the Dean of the College of Arts and Sciences has a suite of offices on the third floor.

To say that the Hall of Languages was gutted would be to understate the case seriously. In order to insert five concrete floors where there had been four of wood, and to accommodate 76 faculty offices and as many as 2,300 students at class time (4,600 between classes), the old floors had to be removed and the old timber columns and most of the interior brick bearing walls replaced with steel. At the same time, the exterior stone walls could not even temporarily bear the weight of the heavy timbered mansard roof and cupolas unassisted by lateral support from the floor joists (reconstruct-

ing the roof with steel was economically impossible). And because the old fourth floor bore the brunt of the roof load on studs, it was, paradoxically, most practical to phase construction from top to bottom, transferring the roof load to the new steel columns via two 12-inch steel channels lag bolted to the wood studs; excess length of stud was snipped off below the new fifth floor when it was complete. The old fourth floor, 4 feet below the new fifth floor, served as a construction platform. (For a graphic description, see preceding page.)

The project was completed within the allotted 15 months—that is, the one school year the faculty felt it could spare the space—and within the $4-million budget, barring a $28 cost overrun.

HALL OF LANGUAGES, Syracuse University, Syracuse, New York. Architects: *Sargent-Webster-Crenshaw & Folley in association with Architectural Resources Cambridge Inc.—Arthur C. Friedel, Jr., AIA, partner-in-charge, Sargent-Webster-Crenshaw & Folley; Colin L. Smith, AIA, Architectural Resources of Cambridge Inc.* Engineers: *Sargent-Webster-Crenshaw & Folley* (structural, soils, mechanical/electrical). Landscape architects: *Carol R. Johnson and Associates.* Construction manager: *J. D. Taylor Construction Corporation.*

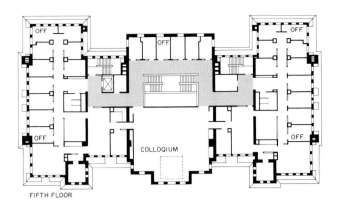

FIFTH FLOOR

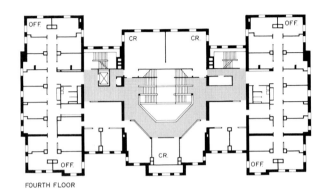

FOURTH FLOOR

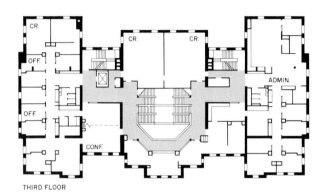

THIRD FLOOR

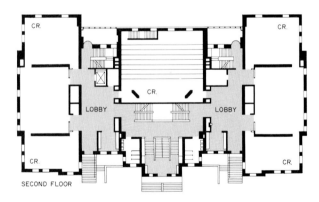

SECOND FLOOR

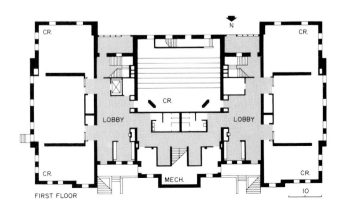

FIRST FLOOR

The stairway at the Hall of Languages, cutting a swath through a series of setbacks, offers climbers a choice of easy flights in two directions at each landing. On the fifth floor, the procession culminates at the Colloquium, a large room for scholarly lectures set below and daylighted by the hall's central tower, which commands a long view of Syracuse through its three arched windows and down the axial street that leads to the front door. Butt glazing between the Colloquium and the stairwell provides auditory protection. Departmental offices—English, Fine Arts, Religion, Philosophy and the Honors Program—occupy the fourth and fifth floors, while the Dean's office and student advisers for the College of Arts and Sciences occupy the third, symbolically accessible to both faculty and students.

© *Nick Wheeler photos*

4
YALE TRANSLATES AN ABANDONED CHAPEL AS A NEW COMMONS

The logotype of Yale's School of Organization and Management is a square ringed about with small circles, representing a table and chairs. As he designed the school's new commons, architect Herbert Newman bore in mind the credo of the school's founding dean, William Donaldson, that conversations held around the dining table are always more rewarding than those conducted around the conference table.

A chapel that had belonged to the Berkeley Divinity School, before Berkeley merged with Yale, houses the commons at a remote corner of the university's campus. One of the primary considerations Newman faced, even as he considered ways to expand the space for kitchen and dining, was its scale on a restricted and peculiar site. The new street facade, which incorporates one end of the chapel, required a residential scale to complement existing buildings in the neighborhood. On the other side of the block and slightly uphill, however, the social sciences library imposed a more institutional scale, as did Hammond Hall, an older building used by the engineering school across the street. To complicate matters still further, the style and materials of the other buildings on the site differed markedly: one middle-aged brick social studies library, one angular dark brick

turn-of-the-century building, and one more recent angular red brick building.

Describing his solution, Newman talks much of Yale's architectural typology and of James Gamble Rogers's large green courtyards, bounded by college walls and entered through low arched portals. Here, the commons establishes a new courtyard, using one crossbar and the stem of the T-shaped building to define the corner. The reference to Rogers's courtyards is clear, despite the architectural variety of the enclosing walls. Instead of entering beneath an arch, the visitor walks in on narrow paths between buildings, a way at once public and pleasantly secretive.

The existing fabric of the chapel has disappeared almost completely on the exterior, enveloped by additions. But the additions, however frankly they announce their contemporaneity, subtly flatter the original and its neighbors with their materials, their scale and their details.

At the corner of the courtyard, the steep pitch of the chapel's low-eaved roof is repeated by the new wing set at a right angle, and the slope of the roof continues across a sensitively proportioned radiused skylight above the dining hall's glass wall. For dining alcoves on the courtyard face of the old chapel, Newman added generous bay win-

Yale's Donaldson Commons, occupying the chapel of a former divinity school and new additions, accommodates the School of Organization and Management. Architect Herbert Newman has used diverse existing buildings and the T-shaped commons to enclose an interior courtyard, a familiar collegiate amenity at Yale. At the same time its artful voids and angles place the building's facade as late 20th-century architecture, its red brick, white wood trim and precast concrete lintels (pigmented and sandblasted to recall older stone) defer to the more mature buildings.

dows whose angular form imitates the bay windows sported by a neighbor, as well as the one on the chapel's street front.

The composition of the new street facade was even trickier than the courtyard.

Newman handled the new wing on the right simply: a plain brick wall with a concrete coping, resembling a domestic garden wall, to enclose the kitchen and food service area. Pedestrians on the street can see over the wall an older, taller building—another of Rogers's favorite devices.

On the left, however, the new building had to resolve the scale of the chapel end with that of a new brick building on the site, a rather tall angular building, formerly a dormitory and now an office building, that Newman says was "unhappy in its solitude" on the corner. With a steep triangular slate roof, the architect leads one's view from a low corner in front to a high diagonal ridge, and then draws the eye still higher as it follows the chimney, until at last it reaches the roof of the building next door.

On the interior of the commons, old and new structures merge without conceding their respective identities. Symmetrical timber trusses support the peaked ridge of the chapel, while the addition, all asymmetry, has diagonal trusses supporting a single-pitched roof to its ridge above the flat front wall. Trusses are exposed on both sides of the L-shaped dining area.

The commons interior design defines a broad array of discrete dining areas, offering freedom of choice among communal refectory, conversation *à deux* along the courtyard windows, select groups in the bay windows, or private lunch meetings in various sized alcoves. One of the cubical "boxes" projected toward the street from the addition can convert to a bar for dinner meetings.

The facility is intended chiefly for student lunches, however, and in its first year of operation has attracted numbers despite its distance from the central campus.

DONALDSON COMMONS, Yale University, New Haven, Connecticut. Architects: *Herbert S. Newman Associates, AIA, P.C.—Herbert S. Newman,* architect-in-charge; *Joseph C. Schiffer, AIA,* associate, project architect; *Barry Svigals; Beck Swanson.* Engineers: *John C. Martin, P.E., Consulting Engineers* (structural); *Peter Szilagyi & Associates* (mechanical/elecrical). Interior design: *Herbert S. Newman Associates, AIA, P.C.* Landscape architects: *Zion & Breen Associates.* Consultants: *Donald L. Bliss* (lighting); *Strong Cohen* (graphics). Cost consultant: *George A. Fuller Co.* General contractor: *The Joseph F. Kelly Co., Inc.*

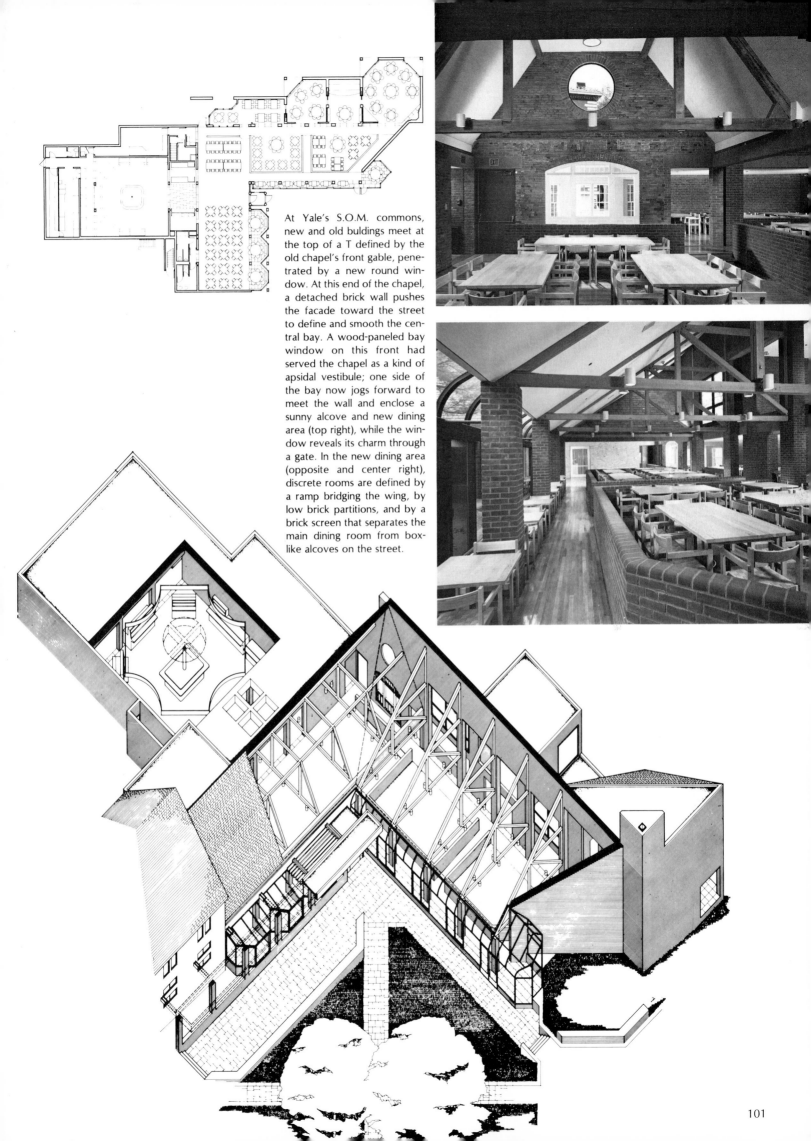

At Yale's S.O.M. commons, new and old buldings meet at the top of a T defined by the old chapel's front gable, penetrated by a new round window. At this end of the chapel, a detached brick wall pushes the facade toward the street to define and smooth the central bay. A wood-paneled bay window on this front had served the chapel as a kind of apsidal vestibule; one side of the bay now jogs forward to meet the wall and enclose a sunny alcove and new dining area (top right), while the window reveals its charm through a gate. In the new dining area (opposite and center right), discrete rooms are defined by a ramp bridging the wing, by low brick partitions, and by a brick screen that separates the main dining room from box-like alcoves on the street.

Norman McGrath photos

5
YALE REMODELS THE OLD CAMPUS—A GREAT LATE-19th-CENTURY LANDMARK

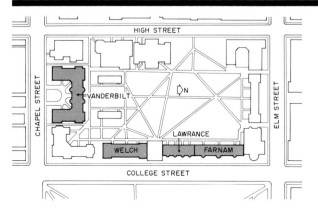

Since the 1930s, Yale's Old Campus has been the home of the freshman class—an enviable group, fortunate in having overcome stiff competition to be admitted to one of the nation's leading universities. Generation after generation has moved into three splendid High-Victorian dormitories—Farnam (1869-70), Durfee (1871), and Lawrance (1885-86) all three designed by Russell Sturgis, Jr; and two fine examples of the English Collegiate style—Welch (1891) by Bruce Price and Vanderbilt Hall (1894) by Charles C. Haight.

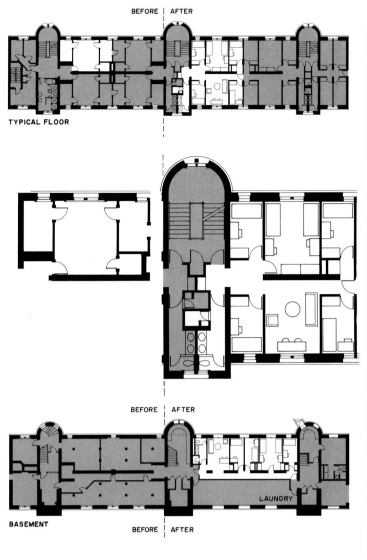

BEFORE | AFTER

TYPICAL FLOOR

BEFORE | AFTER

BEFORE | AFTER

BASEMENT

LAUNDRY

BEFORE | AFTER

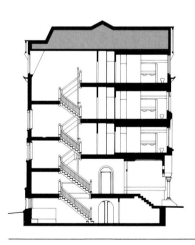

Farnam: The typical floors were gutted to bring the single bedrooms up to the code width of 7 feet. The basement slab and window sills were lowered. The east side of the basement, overlooking the New Haven Green has been developed as suites, and the opposite side as common facilities. The apses in two of the three basement stairwells are used as small living rooms for double suites. The third apse is used as a sitting area for the laundry.

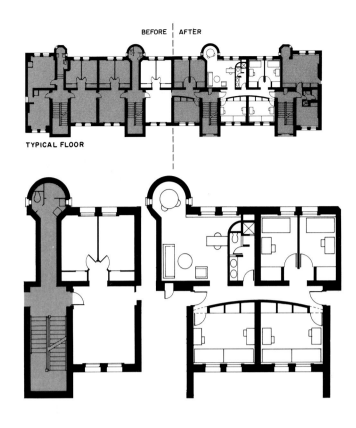

BEFORE | AFTER

TYPICAL FLOOR

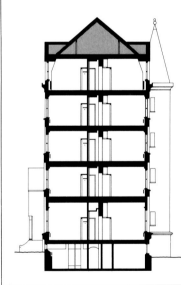

Lawrance: The circular towers once enclosed bathrooms. By removal of the bearing wall, these spaces were incorporated into living rooms and made into sitting alcoves and study niches. The curving wall in the corridor gives a special architectural character to Lawrance while maintaining existing arched brick entries. The basement floor was lowered to gain legal headroom, to make space for mechanical equipment, and to accommodate new suites.

Except for the switch from gas to electric light, the periodic upgrading of plumbing and heating facilities, and general maintenance, these dormitories have been little altered since Farnam was begun. In recent years they have become desperately crowded. Double-decker bunks were crowded into small bedrooms originally designed for one. Up to eight students shared a single toilet, sink and shower in small awkward bathrooms in public hallways. To avoid using double-deckers, many students put their beds in the living rooms of what had grown from two-person to four-person suites, thus destroying what had heretofore been the shared communal space. For the students and their proud parents on moving-in day, only the euphoria generated by making it to Yale can have mitigated the thundering shock delivered by the first look at the tenement-like freshman suites.

Something had to be done. Several years ago a proposal for two new student residential colleges on nearby Whitney Avenue and Grove streets seemed to be the answer. John Hay Whitney of the class of '26 donated 15 million dollars for the proposed buildings and planning began. Fortunately for the cause of extending the life of fine old buildings, the new colleges fell through. The University and the New Haven Board of Aldermen could not agree on a tax financing plan for the project, and the Board refused to approve the construction. By the time this decision was overturned by the courts, building construction costs had become prohibitive. Furthermore, students at Yale and on other campuses were

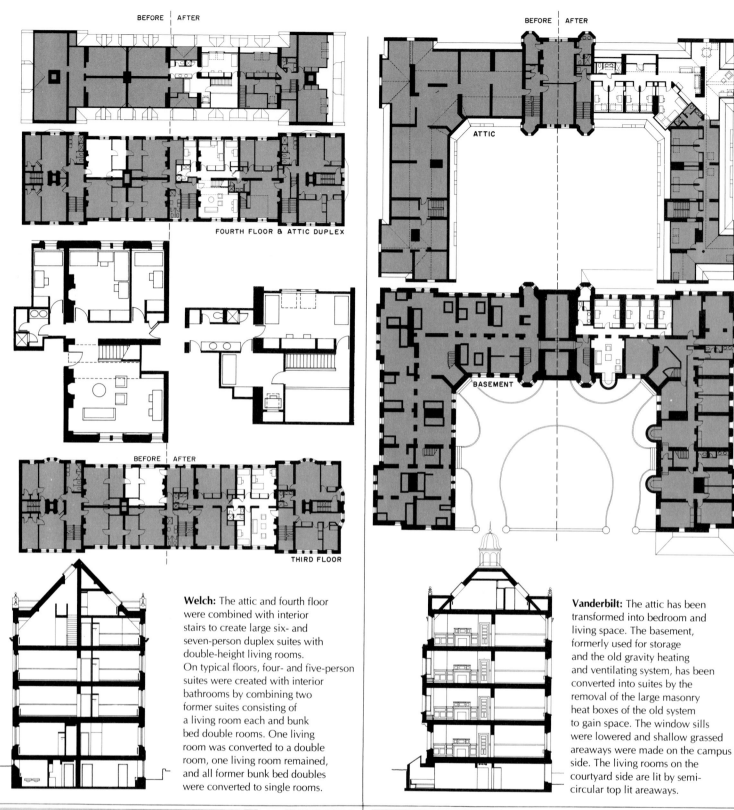

BEFORE | AFTER

FOURTH FLOOR & ATTIC DUPLEX

BEFORE | AFTER

THIRD FLOOR

ATTIC

BEFORE | AFTER

BASEMENT

Welch: The attic and fourth floor were combined with interior stairs to create large six- and seven-person duplex suites with double-height living rooms. On typical floors, four- and five-person suites were created with interior bathrooms by combining two former suites consisting of a living room each and bunk bed double rooms. One living room was converted to a double room, one living room remained, and all former bunk bed doubles were converted to single rooms.

Vanderbilt: The attic has been transformed into bedroom and living space. The basement, formerly used for storage and the old gravity heating and ventilating system, has been converted into suites by the removal of the large masonry heat boxes of the old system to gain space. The window sills were lowered and shallow grassed areaways were made on the campus side. The living rooms on the courtyard side are lit by semi-circular top lit areaways.

Welch Hall from New Haven Green.

Vanderbilt Hall Courtyard.

1

2

beginning to realize how much they loved old buildings and preferred them as places to live. There was little enthusiasm among Yale students for the new residential colleges scheme. As a result of these considerations, Yale's then-president, Kingman Brewster Jr. spent $7.3 million of Whitney's gift on Farnam, Lawrance, Welch, Vanderbilt, Durfee and McClellan including furniture, landscaping, management costs and all fees. The quarters of 1,000 students have been renovated at a cost of $7,000 per bed. (Comparable costs of new construc-

tion in New Haven in 1975 were figured to be $13,000 per bed.)

Brewster established a faculty-student committee headed by associate provost Jonathan Fanton to work with the two associated architectural firms: Edward L. Barnes, Architect, New York City and Herbert S. Newman Associates, New Haven. Every aspect of the renovation, from basic suite arrangements to the design of the storage units under each bed was carefully worked out among the Yale Office of Facilities Planning, the architects and

the committee.

The goal of the renovation was to gain 120 beds and to reduce overcrowding; to bring the buildings up to the current life safety code; to renovate completely the heating, electric and plumbing systems; and to renovate all the building finishes and the structure for long-term dormitory use.

The two architectural firms developed common design objectives for all the buildings to be renovated. First, they determined that the architectural character of each building was to

be preserved as much as possible by retaining the original materials, details and external appearance of the buildings—which when taken as a whole represent a unique period in late 19th century American architecture. Second, they wished to provide a variety of room types and sizes. Third, they decided to provide two means of egress from each suite, accomplished without affecting the privacy of adjacent suites. Fourth, they concluded that the bathrooms should be provided within the suites rather than at public corridors and

The Lawrance typical floor suite corridors (Figure 1), and the basement corridor (Figure 2), both on preceding pages, are punctuated by a series of beautiful brick arches left intact by the architects. The arches have also been retained in the Farnam basement (Figure 6), and throughout the structure. The Farnam entrances (Figure 3) have new glass doors to accentuate the silhouettes of the beautiful pierced-stone transoms as seen from within, and to make the severely handsome character of the brick and tile stairwells visible from without. In the stairwells of Welch (Figure 4), new oak walls conceal emergency devices and utility closets while carrying the building's name and floor identification as an ornamental detail. The steeply pitched roofs in the Vanderbilt attic (Figure 5) make good space.

1

stairhalls. This makes the bathrooms secure from intruders, permits bathroom sundries to be left in the bathrooms, and encourages student maintenance of their own bathrooms.

As planning progressed it was decided that a six-person suite arrangement of four singles, one double, a living room and a private bath shared by all six was the optimum arrangement. This organization of space had to vary in response to the actual conditions existing in each of the old buildings. Wherever possible the architects converted the existing

suites originally designed for two but now containing up to four persons into suites for six. This was done by converting alternate living rooms into double bedrooms, thus permitting the crowded small bedrooms to revert to single occupancy. Although on typical floors, the density increased slightly, a significant number of additional beds were gained by taking over the attics in Vanderbilt and Welch and the basements of Farnam, Lawrance, Welch and Vanderbilt as living quarters. The attics and basements were remodeled with great care to

minimize the effect on the exteriors.

The renovation of the four halls shown began in the spring of 1976 and the buildings were ready for occupancy that fall. Two additional halls including Durfee were ready in the fall of 1977. The freshmen are delighted with their new quarters, which now surpass in spaciousness and esthetic quality most of the residential college living suites of upper classmen including the cramped bedrooms of Eero Saarinen's Morse and Ezra Stiles Colleges (1960-62). Traditionally, when a student

2

3

4

5

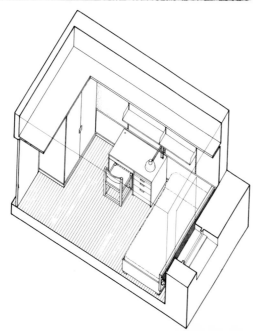

The Welch duplex living room (Figure 1), preceding
page, is part of a suite for 6 to 7 persons.
To achieve this space, the attic and
the fourth floor were combined. The double
bedroom in the Welch duplex (Figure 2)
has windows of the type that were used in all the
attics renovated. Constructed of aluminum-clad
wood and tempered bronze glass they were designed
for installation in a sloping roof surface
with a minimum of disruption to the roof
plane. The window has a reversing mechanism for
exterior glass cleaning. The existing
fenestration was kept intact in all buildings
except for lowering basement sills or
replacing sash, glazing and trim where
necessary. Farnam is the only building with
all new window trim (Figures 4 and 5).
The existing trim in Lawrance (Figure 3)
was left as is. Fully furnished mock-up rooms
containing the elements shown in the isometric
were carefully analyzed.

leaves the Old Campus, he moves up to better quarters. If this is to continue, Yale will either have to upgrade many more student rooms, or put its seniors back on the Old Campus, which once, long ago, was their preserve.

YALE UNIVERSITY OLD CAMPUS RENOVATION PHASE ONE: FARNAM, LAWRANCE, WELCH, VANDERBILT HALLS, New Haven, Connecticut. Owner: *Yale University.* Architects for Farnam and Vanderbilt: *Edward L. Barnes, Architect—Edward Z.*

Jacobsen, associate; Thomas V. Czarnowski and Frederick Stelle, project architects; Mary Barnes, interior design. Architects for Lawrance and Welch: *Herbert S. Newman Associates—Glenn Gregg, partner, Don Cosham and Joseph Schiffer, project architects; Monique M. Corbat-Brooks, Robert Gotshall, Susan Marko and Neil Troiano, assistants.* Consultants: *Spiegel & Zamecnik* (structural /foundation engineers); *Yale University Engineering Services* (mechanical); *Zion & Breen* (landscape); *George A. Fuller Co.* (costs); *Glendon R. Mayo* (building code). General contractor: *E. & F. Construction Co.*

A typical basement living room in Vanderbilt (Figure 1) is lit by a top-lighted circular areaway, which meets the light and ventilation requirements with a minimum of disruption to the landscaping and architectural character of the Vanderbilt courtyard. The circular seating area (Figure 2) is in a basement apse in Farnam. The second floor living room in Lawrance (Figure 3) extends into the turret, formerly occupied by an inadequate toilet facility. As already mentioned, the furnishing of the student bedrooms was done by the university according to mock-ups carefully studied by the architects, the students and the university management. The living rooms, however, have been exuberantly furnished by the suite occupants themselves, with the traditional reliance upon the New Haven flea markets.

6
YALE ADAPTS ITS LAW SCHOOL LIBRARY AND LECTURE HALL FOR TODAY'S STUDENT LIFESTYLE

Architects Herbert Newman Associates were chosen by their clients from the Yale Law School because of their previous sensitivity in renovating the dormitories of Yale's Old Campus. And sensitivity was clearly a primary component of the success of these two similar-but-different remodelings with the venerable Law School building—especially if the original elegance was to be reasserted. When the school first occupied the buildings in 1932, there were only 330 students. And, as Associate Dean Arthur Charpentier states, it was a time of different fashions, technologies and—perhaps most important—different life-styles. In the library, students were expected to sit in quiet rows at communal tables, and to take noisier pursuits and lounging postures back to nearby dormitory rooms.

Today, there are almost twice the number of students, and two thirds of this unanticipated throng live off campus—some at considerable distances. Before the remodelings, the lecture hall was arranged in "old-style authoritarian"—with tables rigidly facing a speaker at the distant narrow end of the room. The library furnishings had grown shabby, and there was noise and confusion from such unforeseen electronic equipment as duplicators and microphotographic machines.

In not so distant times, such obviously inadequate facilities might have called for a new building, but—as more and more often seems appropriate in these times—the faculty and the alumni settled on the course of renovation of their memorable spaces. And accordingly, Herbert Newman Associates have given them what might have been thought to be the impossible: facilities within the old visual and spatial confines that meet today's greatly changed and expanded needs.

Robert Perron photos

THE LECTURE HALL

This room underwent a complete reorientation—to place the speaker (and new audio-visual aids) in the center of the long wall, and hence to improve both the visual and acoustical relationships of speaker to students. Seating was placed on new stepped and curved platforms to further improve the relationships. While as many elements of the old room (left) as possible were kept (such as the handsome oak wainscoting and doors), new elements were added—such as the dropped beams that conceal lighting and the handsome new furnishings.

THE YALE UNIVERSITY LIBRARY AND LECTURE HALL, New Haven, Connecticut. Architects: *Herbert S. Newman Associates*—partner-in-charge: *Herbert Newman*; project architect: *Glenn H. Gregg*. Engineers: *John C. Martin* (structural); *Yale Engineering Services* (electrical). Consultants: *Sylvan R. Shemitz Associates* (lighting in library); *Donald Bliss* (lighting in lecture hall). Contractors: *E+P Construction Company* (library); *Megin Construction Company* (lecture hall).

LAW SCHOOL LIBRARY

It has been since its opening in 1932 one of the more elegant and opulent spaces at the University—despite an incrustation of makeshift equipment and lighting (photo below). It was clearly a space worthy of preservation. Accordingly, Herbert Newman Associates' approach to meeting the demands of many new uses was to actually restore the shell of the space with its rich detailing; while shifting the congesting and inappropriate equipment (such as photocopying and microphotographic machines) into adjacent spaces. Also out of the room went the long reading tables (except for one in each of the two seating groups at the far ends). In their place came a combination of task-ambient-lit oak carrels and comfortable chairs for reading—while lounging per se was relegated to a niche beside the main desk (photo above) that once held the card catalogs. The card catalogs were relocated to the center of the room for easier visibility and access. Another major visual change was Sylvan Shemitz Associates' combination of up- and down-lighting that replaces the hanging fixtures, which obscured the grandeur of the room. This design radically changes the character of the room at night (see photo).

In the early design stages, the architects displayed a model of the room and a mock-up study carrel for suggestions, and some of the student comments were incorporated in the final plans. The work had to be compressed into a period between the beginning of June and the following Labor Day—a tough schedule that *was* met (despite a maintenance employees' strike) by prefabrication of the various elements. The room has been so successful that the librarians are constantly having to discourage use by students from outside the Law School, and Dean Charpentier refers to this circumstance as "an odd by-product of success."

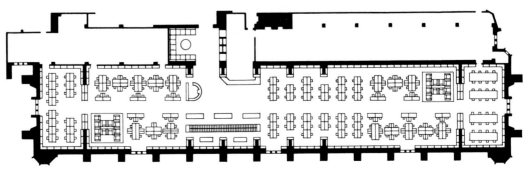

4

Architects are not the only business people who like to do their work surrounded by 19th-century industrial mill construction, neoclassic cabinet work and moldings, Victorian jigsaw fretwork, or small domestic interiors. Although two of the projects shown in this chapter have been designed by architects for themselves, the rest of the workplaces have been adapted for cranberry merchants, a newspaper staff, a suburban dentist, savings bank personnel and their customers, administrators of the Harvard Business School, a consul for the Ivory Coast, and an antique dealer.

The growing popularity of recycling the odd or curious building for business use is of course rooted in economics — such buildings are often in cheaper neighborhoods and cost less to buy or rent. Just as important, however, is the growing dislike, by the kinds of people who tend to be smaller entrepreneurs, of the newness, slickness, and lack of character of most newly built office space. Such people often seem to prefer the old and handmade as a counterpoint to the technological sophistication of their own enterprises.

The owners of Ocean Spray Cranberries, for example, decided to combine new office space with an indoor-outdoor exhibit of their product. They picked Plymouth, Massachusetts, for its harbor, its history, and its tourists, and found an abandoned clam processing plan to remodel into the office and exhibit space. Surrounded by brand new cranberry bogs, installed for educational purposes, the old plant suggests 19th-century craft—an exercise in nostalgia which must favor sales of cranberries actually produced by not so picturesque late 20th-century methods.

The printing plant and office of a newspaper in Russellville, Kentucky, is housed in a 19th-century feed and hardware store. Enough of the old structure—brick bearing walls, cast iron columns, and old floor planks — has been preserved and adapted to remind the newspaper staff and customers of the humble, yet sturdy enterprises of their forefathers, enhancing their own public image.

OFFICES,
SHOWROOMS
AND A BANK

A dentist in Woodstock, New York, has turned a small house into a suite of dental offices, deliberately domestic in character. Here, too, the use of an old building with its own warm and friendly connotations creates an atmosphere which somewhat ameliorates the experience in the dentist's chair.

Some of the older buildings in this chapter have been appropriately recycled, not because the original structure necessarily enhances the owner/tenant image, but simply because the site or functional considerations demanded the transformation. The East Cambridge Savings Bank in Cambridge, Massachusetts, was always a distinguished and elegant banking structure, its granite, marble, and bronze proper symbols of richness and probity. Because the building no longer served the increasingly complex spatial requirements of modern banking, it has been remodelled in startling fashion.

Other renovations in this category are the administrative offices in Glass Hall at the Harvard Business School, the Consulate for the Ivory Coast in New York City, and the G.S. McKenna Gallery in Charlotte, North Carolina.

Of the two adaptations by architects for themselves, the first building, at Redondo Beach, California, was remodeled largely because of its suitable size and location for a combined architect's office and showroom. The second building is an architect's dream — a granite office structure built between 1890 and 1892 by Shepley, Rutan and Coolidge. It has a wonderful 75-foot diameter rotunda on the top floor under a cone-shaped dome. Its new occupants, Jung/Brannen Associates have created a light and graceful multi-level work space in bright and airy juxtaposition to the solid granite Romanesque hall which contains it. Here the power of the 19th-century enclosure reminds architect and visiting client alike what architecture once was, a valuable lesson for those who struggle to shape what it will be.

1
RENOVATION-ADDITION TO HISTORIC WATERFRONT SITE

Every summer, visitors by the hundreds of thousands stream into Plymouth, often as part of a three-day tour of Cape Cod and the historic districts of eastern Massachusetts. They visit the Rock itself, the landmark houses and museums, and most stroll the deck of the Mayflower II which is tied up at quayside. Now there is a new attraction—an attraction open to all, but perhaps especially welcome to parents of youngsters with parched throats and attention spans that are beginning to fail. It is the renovated headquarters of Ocean Spray Cranberries, Incorporated. It occupies what had been a processing building for the local clamming industry and it sits, not surprisingly, in a sea of transplanted cranberry bogs. Allen Moore Jr., of Moore-Heder, Architects, managed the renovation/addition that includes exhibit spaces both inside and out. The exterior exhibits, spaced apart on a broad visitors deck at bogside, mix refreshment with history and cranberry lore. They are interesting and informative. Other more fragile exhibits with similar themes continue inside.

Beyond these gracious public spaces, which are of course designed to have significant public relations value, are the office spaces that form the Cooperative's administrative core. These are grouped in the existing, refaced structure and the new 26,000-square-foot addition. The offices are arranged in an open plan with a system of half-height partitions designed by the architect. Task lighting in the form of 2- by 4-foot suspended panels is augmented by general illumination from pendant fixtures that have been modified to fluorescent and, in the new wing, by daylighting from a double-height atrium space. Old wall finishes were replaced with sheet rock, the timber roof structure exposed, reinforced, and fitted with new roof decking. Both renovated and new exterior construction, including glazing, was insulated carefully and the project is protected by a new sprinkler system.

The renovation derives much of its success from its simplicity and from the sympathetic handling of wood and brick. The new is grafted to the old directly and without any apparent fussiness of detail, and both are unified by the handsome outdoor spaces.

OCEAN SPRAY CRANBERRIES, INC., Plymouth, Massachusetts. Architects: *Moore-Heder*, Cambridge. Developer: *Julius Tofias & Company, Inc.* Engineers: *Engineer's Design Group* (structural); *Wayne Peterson Associates* (mechanical); *Verne Norman Associates* (electrical). Interior consultants: *Gardiner Associates*. Contractor: *Peabody Construction Company, Inc.*

All bog planting was accomplished by members of the Cooperative who transplanted working vines for the first time ever in order to shorten the time—usually three years—to maturity. These bogs are worked as part of the educational displays.

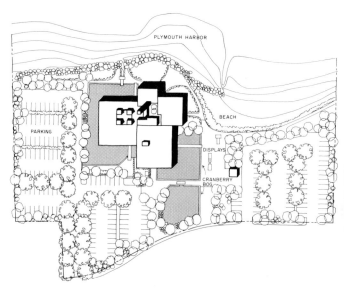

The interior partitioning system, designed by the architects, was competitive with conventional systems to build and install, and furthermore reflects the wood trim and wall finishes of the balance of the building. Electrical and telephone cables are carried "piggyback" in wood saddles over the duct distribution system. Metal fins are used as required as static barriers in the saddles to separate power and telephone lines.

2
A FEED AND HARDWARE STORE RECYCLED INTO A NEWSPAPER OFFICE AND PRINTING PLANT

Happily for the community of Russellville, Kentucky, the publisher of several local newspapers decided to expand his offices and printing plant in one of the few remaining nineteenth century buildings on the town square. The architects, Ryan, Cooke & Zuern, were asked to study the feasibility of recycling several sites on the square to provide current and future production space. Of some importance was the client's wish that the production of his publications be a visible part of the square's activity. The project was to include 7000 square feet of finished, air-conditioned, expandable space—for under $100,000.

The selected location was a combined feed and hardware store that had endured the usual ''modernizations.'' Its advantages—besides a prominent location on the square—included adjacent off-street parking, and a structure that offered positive separation of production and publication functions.

The street facade was stripped of years of various remodelings, revealing the original cast-iron and brick structure. These elements were restored and infilled with woodwork that duplicates the spirit of original doors and trim found stored in the cellar.

The two-story hardware store now houses the publication edi-

torial, circulation, advertising and management spaces, using an open-office design for immediate convertibility.

The one-story feed store was reworked to accommodate the pressroom and mailroom. Expansion of these two areas will occur in new space erected on the adjoining parking lot.

In the renovation, the existing masonry load-bearing structure could be used. The poplar floors of the feed store were removed and a new concrete slab poured on engineered fill for the presses. The floor boards and structural members were then reused for partition paneling and new stair construction. Plaster was removed from brick walls which were cleaned and left exposed. Existing wood floors and ceilings were simply cleaned, and new mechanical, electrical and sprinkler systems were installed throughout.

Outside, overhead utility lines and lighting were removed from the street facade, and the crumbling walk was replaced with new concrete and brick paving. Street trees were also added.

PRINTING PLANT AND OFFICE FOR THE LOGAN LEADER/THE NEWS DEMOCRAT, Russellville, Kentucky. Owner: *Logan Ink Inc.* Architects: *Ryan, Cooke and Zuern Associates Inc.* Contractor: *Logan Ink Inc.*

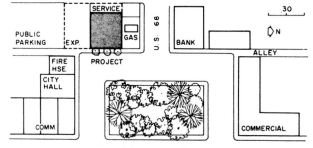

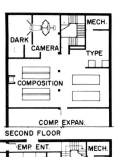

SECOND FLOOR

One half of the second floor remains unassigned as expansion for the composition room and a self-contained news room. When this expansion occurs, the street floor will be reassigned for those business and administrative tasks directly involving the public.

Balthazar Korab photos

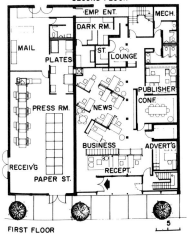

FIRST FLOOR

5

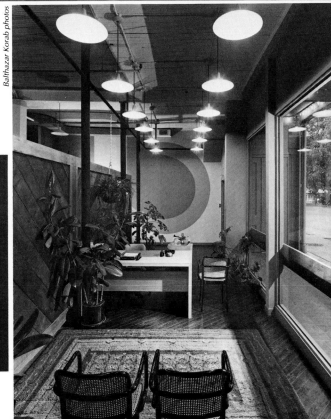

A SUBURBAN PREFAB HOUSE CONVERTED INTO DENTAL OFFICES

These dental offices, which are an example of the maximum effect with the minimum of means, began life in 1965 as a plain prefabricated one-family house built on a site at the intersection of two important roads in Woodstock. Because of its site, and because its basic shell was sound, it was reconstructed for its new use, though almost the only remnant of its domestic past that is still visible is its over-all volume and its characteristically suburban low-pitched gable roof. The inside of the building was gutted, and new interior partitions were erected; the outside was reclad with cedar siding. Three important elements were involved in the new plan: a new entrance from the adjacent parking lot, a central gallery through the length of the building and connecting all of the rooms, and a bay window at the far end of the gallery. What results is something economically special, a linear pathway from the car to the entrance, pausing inside in a waiting room, then moving from it to one of the dentists' offices beyond, with the bay window serving as an ultimate termination of the route. All of this is carefully configured and carefully, though simply, detailed. The front walk, the vestibule floor, and a part of the waiting room floor are of bluestone. The ceilings in the waiting room and in the dentists' offices are made of cypress slats, and in the latter spaces they are placed on the diagonal to the walls. In the waiting room and the long gallery, the wall surfaces are of vinyl-covered linen, and in the offices and other spaces they are of vinyl. Floors, aside from the main entrance, are of carpet or tile. The effect of all this is clear, quiet, and soothing, an environment designed to make the best of what can for many people, adults and children alike, be an anxious experience. Thoughtful touches include the fact that each of the dentists' chairs has a carefully composed view of the outdoors, and the two offices at the end of the building have views through the bay window as well by virtue of their little corner windows. Again, all of this seems achieved without much architectural strain, and without rhetoric.

DENTAL OFFICES, Woodstock, New York. Architects: *R. M. Kliment and Frances Halsband.* General contractor: *Roy H. Hoffman.*

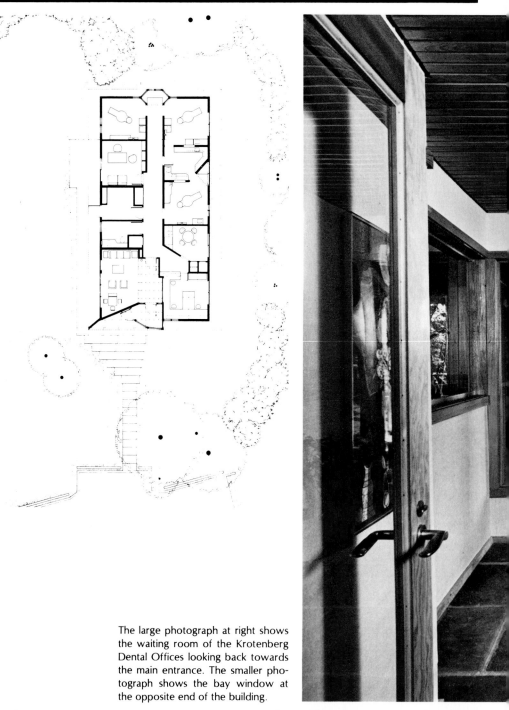

The large photograph at right shows the waiting room of the Krotenberg Dental Offices looking back towards the main entrance. The smaller photograph shows the bay window at the opposite end of the building.

Norman McGrath photos

4

MINOR ALTERATIONS PRODUCE A NEW WORKING ENVIRONMENT WITHIN A NEO-GEORGIAN HOUSE AT HARVARD

Notable for producing a major change with one relatively modest structural innovation, this remodeling for the administrative offices of the Harvard Graduate School of Business Administration has, as its central focus, a narrow light well cut through the two upper floors. As a result, all of the activities, related by function, are related visually as well. The key to the design's success lies in the sensitive way in which the proportions of the well relate to the interior space as a whole, and help to unify the interior as one large volume. The architects have opened a closed box by the simplest of means.

Formerly a warren of offices, the three floors are in a building designated by the master plan of McKim, Mead & White as faculty housing. The building, built in 1927, lends a special charm to the quadrangle of which it is an integral part, and the lack of exterior alteration is a particular tribute to intelligent planning. Much of the floor areas within are now open, without partitions. And where new partitions were required, they were handled with particular skill—as in the case of the translucent-glass enclosure at the bottom of the well, which admits ''borrowed'' light while maintaining privacy. The well was accomplished with less than an eight-percent loss of the original floor area. The well and the deft handling of the other new major elements have created a successful, totally contemporary and workable environment, while respecting the old building.

GLASS HALL, HARVARD BUSINESS SCHOOL, Cambridge, Massachusetts. Owner: *The President and Fellows of Harvard College*. Architects: *SZB Associates, Inc.—architects: Ilhan Zeybekoglu and Vincent Solomita; job captain: Eric Ward*. Engineers: *Souza and True Inc.* (structural); *Progressive Consulting Engineers* (mechanical); *Metcalf Engineering* (electrical). General contractor: *Minton Construction Company*.

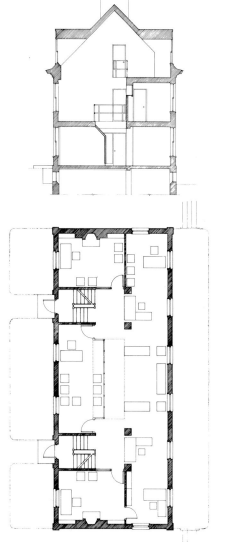

5
TRANSFORMATION OF A NEW YORK TOWNHOUSE INTO A CONTEMPORARY CONSULATE

Architect Susana Torre is so strongly influenced by the basic nature of every building for which she designs interiors that she makes this nature an integral part of her expressive design language. For this consulate in New York City, Torre designed two very different schemes for two very different successive buildings. And the results graphically illustrate both how she is influenced by the buildings, and what she means when she says that—despite the obvious design differences that come from context—she has "a constant theory of interior space. There are three parallel considerations that lead to both proper formal relationships and the tensions that are important to make the viewer aware of environment." (And more subtle than to seem contrived, the tensions are "neither

purely perceptual nor conceptual.") The parallel considerations are structure (the actual and what Torre wants the viewer to perceive), the hierarchies of activity (which if properly arranged produce a certain sense of ceremony) and the purely esthetic and symbolic values. To produce esthetic and symbolic values that are "neither banal or superficial," Torre does extensive research into the natures of her clients, and—in the case of interiors—into the natures of their buildings.

Torre designed two schemes for the Ivory Coast Consulate. Her first design for space in an office building (shown in isometric only) was unexecuted because more suitable quarters were subsequently found. In the first design, the rhythm of columns was expressed by both a series of storage walls and over-

Dorothy Alexander

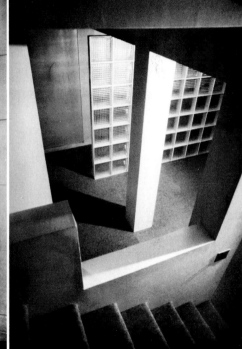

Dorothy Alexander

The entrance area (top right) forms a subtle transition from the symmetry of the facade to a new symmetry that expresses the desire for continued formality and ceremony. At the same time the transition accommodates the asymmetrical stairs and service entrance, located behind the glass-block wall. The ceremonial aspects are strengthened by the symbolic columns (see text) and by a series of walls across the building that are treated like gates, a carryover from an earlier scheme for a different building (see isometric below).

head lighting strips, indefinitely extended by mirrors, through which the visitor would pass in a processional route to reach the offices of the ambassador and financial officer (left in isometric). A semicircular wall around the conference room intrudes into the route, and this was to have been covered in mosaic tile patterned on native weavings. (To learn the code meanings of the weavings, Torre consulted with a historian at Harvard.) Natural light for secretaries—a particular concern of the designers—was to be brought to their cubicles through clear glass block. In the open anonymous framework, the formal concepts take place in concert with structural clues.

The executed design (above, opposite page and overleaf) for the turn-of-the-century townhouse has as its ''structure'' the exist-

ing walls and mechanical enclosures to the right of the plan. While the interiors had been totally altered in recent years and were in bad shape, Torre had a very limited budget. On the typical upper floors, the spaces have been modestly restructured by color and some new construction in the core areas, which are divided into zones by a dark green area across the building at the elevator (see overleaf). Indeed, all of the walls across the building have been treated as gates in a procession. While side walls are white, the cross walls are various colors influenced by both Ivory Coast painters and the building itself. For instance, the front interior walls are a red-tan that matches a color frequently used by the native painters, and the building's brick facade as well. Other gradations of

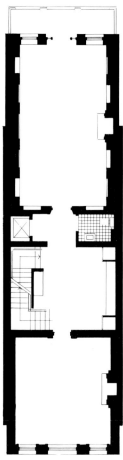

SECOND FLOOR

color are even more subtle, like the palest of sky blues on the ceiling.

The most graphic example of both Torre's "constant theory" and her care about context is the ground-floor reception area. As seen in the photo at right, it seems to be a calmly ordered procession from the entrance. But, a view in the other direction (photos on previous pages) reveals it to be a highly complex sequence of ceremonial "gates." The second gate (inside the street door) is both a sympathetic transfer of symmetry from the facade and a symbol of entering a different culture. The columns' yellow and blue colors, for example, are used at all entrances to symbolize respectively the male and female. Part of the design problem here was to shrink the scale of the space seen on

entry from the larger street facade without losing a sense of importance, and the gates have admirably done this. The glass block wall required to separate the service from the public entries enhances the play of natural light for both visitors and the secretaries, while the dark green wall begins the rhythm of interior divisions that stretch through the building.

CONSULAR AND FINANCIAL OFFICES OF THE EMBASSY OF THE IVORY COAST, New York, New York. Architects: *Susana Torre, The Architectural Studio—production: Dorothy Alexander with Richard Velsor, Steve Midohuas, Jane McGroarty.* Engineers: *Robert Stilman Associates* (structural); *William A. Schwartz and Sons* (mechanical). General contractor: *Garson-Bergman.*

FIRST FLOOR

6
A LOCAL LANDMARK BECOMES AN ARCHITECT'S OFFICE AND FURNITURE SHOWROOM

Synthesis, a confederation of seven young architects, along with the owner of the Ambienti furniture store have sympathetically remodeled the 1925-vintage offices of Southern California Edison in Redondo Beach, California, for their own use. They share the space in an informal way that is not uncommon in Europe. And what may seem to Americans to be an unusual marriage of functions, coupled with the imagery of the resulting interiors, seems particularly appropriate for both the high quality Italian furniture sold and for the way that the architects pursue their work in the widely ranging areas of design, urban planning and environmental research. For the quality of these spaces, the informal arrangement meant that there could be large open areas, with the resulting grand scale that

seems to match the building's character so perfectly. Of course, the marriage also meant that the re-use of the 6,600 square feet of floor space became economically feasible for both groups.

Store owner Fran Mello has a particular fondness for the building, having grown up only a few blocks away. She is the wife of Synthesis architect Daniel Mello, and she can remember when the show windows displayed refrigerators. Now they display elegantly designed furniture in a way that is meant to attract both retail and wholesale interest. And this interest obviously works out to be at least partially symbiotic, as the architects design with Ambienti in mind and the store's customers seek design services. The building is part of the last remaining commer-

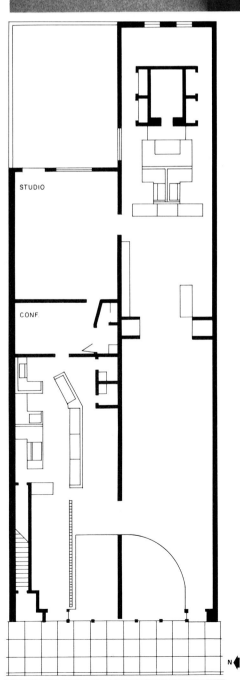

cial block of largely residential Redondo Beach, and—as such—is sort of a landmark. A structural wall down the center forms two roughly equal divisions of the space, which are utilized by having the architects' reception area and some of their desks in the front part of the left hand section, as seen in the plan. A glass-block wall (photos above) funnels visitors past the furniture displays that overlap into this section immediately inside the show window. A small conference room is shared by showroom and designers, and a large workshop and storage room opens to a rear patio. On the right hand side of the plan, the major showroom space is in the front, and a library and design studio (above) is arranged so that both architects and retail personnel can work at the large table with clients.

Here, the original white glazed brick vault where Edison customer payments were kept becomes a central design focus, and serves for storage. Throughout all of the spaces a contrast of textures has been achieved by alternately exposing the structural brick walls and by painstakingly applying a surface of hard plaster. In the rear one-story section, skylights provide natural light over the individual desks.

AMBIENTI/SYNTHESIS, Redondo Beach, California. Architects: *Synthesis—Cheryl Brantner, Daniel Mello, Guido Misculin.* Landscape consultant: *Ron Serrato.* Contractors: *Frances Mello* (general); *Murray Harreschou* (finish carpentry); *Paul Hebert, Bon-Am Enterprises* (plastering).

STUDIO

CONF.

N

7
A CIRCULAR MEZZANINE IN A ROOFTOP ROTUNDA BECOMES AN ARCHITECT'S OFFICES

These architects have taken maximum visual advantage of a wonderful old large-scale rotunda, while gracefully accommodating the many necessary small-scale furnishings that their office functions require. Reception, resource files, meeting areas, drafting tables, and private offices are all located with minimal intrusion in what had been the board room of the old Boston Chamber of Commerce building—a formidable granite structure built between 1890 and 1892 to designs by architects Shepley, Rutan & Coolidge (drawing above).

When the architects moved in, the soaring 75-foot-diameter space had been truncated by the construction of a new floor for a previous tenant at the original visitors'-mezzanine level. But despite the lost height, the room was just the sort of impressive "found dividend" that such older buildings can yield. In order to produce the required floor area and to get as many people near windows as possible, a new mezzanine—containing some twenty drafting tables around the room's circumference—became a frank insertion in a "technological" idiom. Meanwhile, original details, such as the oak-trimmed arch at the entrance (small photo at right) were restored to express the unique nature of the original space. Resource files and a conference and display area occupy the great open center of the room (small, left-hand photo on the opposite page)—replacing a warren of partitions and cubicles set up by the previous tenants. Jung/Brannen are to be commended for the sympathetic way in which they have reinforced existing character with not only an open, radial arrangement of elements, but also with an appropriate palette of sophisticated finishes and textures.

THE OFFICES OF JUNG/BRANNEN ASSOCIATES INC. Architects: *Jung/Brannen Associates*. Engineers: *Paul J. Weidlinger Associates* (structural); *Barstow Engineering Inc.* (mechanical/electrical). General contractor: *Bowdin Construction*.

Peter Vanderwarker photos

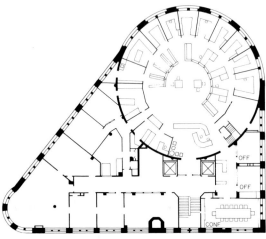

8
MODEST MATERIALS TRANSFORM A HUMBLE SPACE INTO A SETTING FOR ELEGANT ANTIQUES

This small shop is in a very ordinary setting—the space previously housed a budget-clothing emporium in a hodgepodge strip of stores set behind a parking space on a busy street in suburban Charlotte. It is the kind of space that occurs along Main Streets everywhere—but which, alas, seldom gets any kind of design attention. This design serves as a splendid example of what can be done from such modest beginnings—with a very modest budget but a lot of design thought and skill.

The 1800-square-foot building—25 feet wide, 71 feet deep, and 12 feet high—was first stripped bare. The walls and structural columns were painted white; the maple floors (one quality feature that came with the building) refinished; and the ceiling tiles patched or replaced and painted a deep balsam green. A series of nine-foot-high partitions are placed so that they successfully suggest varied fragments of large rooms—suitable settings for the moderately priced antique furniture, paintings and porcelain, and Oriental rugs on sale. A hint of "stately Southern home" is suggested by the detailing of the partitions (all managed with stock moldings and shapes) and the procession of colors used—lime green for one "room," peach for the next, and pale yellow. Where the partitions stop, they are simply sheared off and the ends painted the balsam green of the ceiling; separating and "framing" the room settings, yet relating all of the settings to the total space. The partitions are 2x6 studs and drywall; the spotlighting, porcelain fixtures in a stock steel channel; the fluorescents left exposed. These simple means and materials held the cost of the project, including all fees, to $8 per square foot.

The "worm's eye" perspective shows the simple store front—the sign has a balsam green background with lettering and a stripe (which turns up to mark the entrance) in the same peach and yellow used inside. Designer Gerald Allen has made it all seem very simple and spare and at the same time very elegant—which is, of course, a very difficult kind of design.

G. S. McKENNA GALLERY, Charlotte, N. C. Architects: *Gerald Allen for Peter Gluck & Associates.* General contractor: *Russ Jones Realty and Construction Co.*

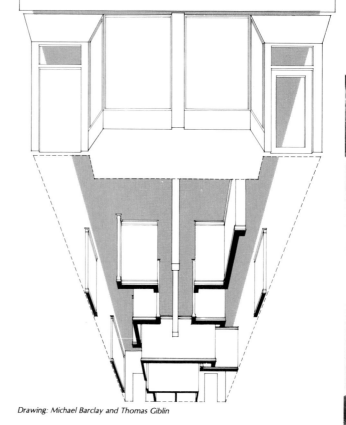

Drawing: Michael Barclay and Thomas Giblin

Photos: Gordon H. Schenk, Jr.

9
A SURPRISING ADDITION
TO A LANDMARK BANK

Similar to many older single-purpose buildings ranging from court-houses to stores, the East Cambridge Savings Bank is a familiar and distinctive landmark that might have been demolished because it was no longer adequate for the increasing complications and magnitude of its functions—even while arousing strong, possibly passionate sentiments in its owners, clients and passers-by. Fortunately, the irreplaceable qualities of such older buildings are being increasingly appreciated, and the decision—when function falters these days—may not be so much whether to tear down and start over as it is how to add on or alter without wrecking the imagery that was so valuable in the first place. Accordingly, the recent work of Charles Hilgenhurst & Associates in adapting this bank to new roles becomes an object lesson in adding on successfully. The elegant Byzantine

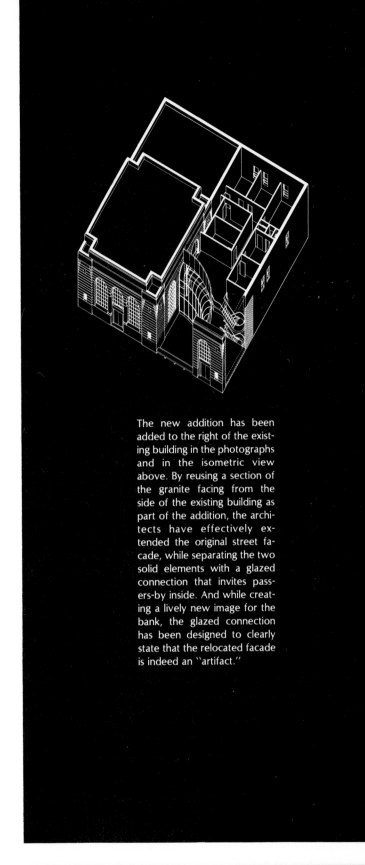

The new addition has been added to the right of the existing building in the photographs and in the isometric view above. By reusing a section of the granite facing from the side of the existing building as part of the addition, the architects have effectively extended the original street facade, while separating the two solid elements with a glazed connection that invites passers-by inside. And while creating a lively new image for the bank, the glazed connection has been designed to clearly state that the relocated facade is indeed an "artifact."

Revival landmark was optimistically built with the richest of materials—granite, marble, and bronze—at the height of the Great Depression in 1931. And its symmetrical form would have seemed to be complete in itself, so that no addition could be an improvement. But the architects have indeed enhanced the old building both by contrast in opening once-rather-somber interiors into bright new spaces and by carrying the current vogue for historical recall one step further. As can be seen in the photos above and right, the straightforward new construction is partially contained within a section of the older building's side facade that has been pushed forward to the street—a section that would have been covered by the new construction. And the wonderful composition that has resulted clearly enhances the visual importance of the whole bank, *and* the original part as well.

Commissioned to almost double by 9,000 square feet the size of the existing structure to accommodate staff offices and mortgage facilities, the architects not only met the requirements admirably, but provided a new, more accessible public image in that part of the addition that faces the street. By connecting the old facade and its relocated offspring with a recessed and lightly framed glass and plastic wall in such a way that the form of the older building keeps its three-dimensional character, the architects have also softened a once-formidable image by inviting the eyes of the passers-by into the new double height public reception area. To facilitate the relocation of the granite facing, the architects located the original quarry, which supplied the 50-year-old stonecutters' drawings. The new curved transparent wall is framed with steel mullions cut from half-inch-thick steel plate—with glass in wall sections, acrylic in the skylight. The structure is steel attached to the steel frame of the old building. The project has received an Award of Excellence from the American Institute of Steel Construction. Construction costs were $500,000 or approximately $48 per square foot, and have saved an irreplaceable building at any cost.

THE EAST CAMBRIDGE SAVINGS BANK, Cambridge, Massachusetts. Architects: *Charles G. Hilgenhurst & Associates—principal-in-charge: Charles Hilgenhurst; associate-in-charge: Robert Silver; design architects: Warren Schwartz, Robert Silver, William Buckingham; project manager: George Fisher; staff: Barbara Ford and William Powell.* Engineers: *Simpson, Gumpertz & Heger* (structural); BR + A (mechanical/electrical). General contractor: *Bond Brothers Incorporated.*

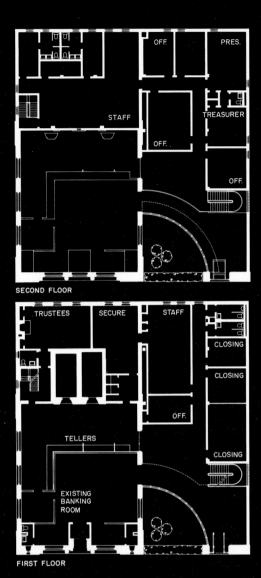

SECOND FLOOR

FIRST FLOOR

To accommodate functions that did not exist or were far less important when the original structure was built, the new addition provides a series of enclosed spaces behind a grand new reception area (photo left) that is an invitation to enter when passers-by look through the new curving glass wall. (Note the sympathetic way in which this wall meets the arched opening in what was the original outside wall.) The meticulously restored banking room is seen below.

5

As long ago as 1889, when Parisians first thronged a restaurant perched upon one of the upper platforms of the Eiffel Tower, people liked to dine out in unlikely places. Because we still do, all kinds of objects get recycled into restaurants: abandoned box cars, cabooses and streetcars; houseboats, stern-wheelers, and barges. All kinds of buildings are eligible too, old windmills, granaries, powder mills, garrisons, saloons, stables, train stations, banks — even churches.

The first trick in adapting such structures, of course, is to create efficient kitchen space and sybaritic dining areas which are nevertheless in the spirit of the rude, honest vernacular in which they are inserted. The second trick is to do all this without destroying the character of the original space itself.

Two successful solutions to this problem are included in this chapter. The first is the Millcroft Inn, Alton, Ontario. Here the architects have inserted multi-level dining spaces into an old mill built in 1881. They have selected contemporary details, such as wood block partitions and simple handrails, which are very much in keeping with the spirit of the old building. The mill construction, left intact, is visible throughout the dining area. The exterior details are of thick stone with deep window reveals. The building looks and feels as old and simple as it is, yet the restaurant, by contrast, is elegant. Another such success is the chic little

RESTAURANTS

eatery in the former baggage room of the 19th-century railroad station in Katonah, New York.

The four remaining projects included in this chapter have in common only the fact that they all occupy buildings which are not new. The restaurant in the Bear Mountain Inn, north of New York City, was always a handsome restaurant space. The re-design is noteworthy because the architects didn't spoil what they had, but successfully reinforced the upstate mountain lodge look of the place.

The St. Francis Yacht Club in San Francisco, built in 1928, virtually burned down in 1976. Again the important task was to rebuild the club in its original character. Restaurant facilities in the style of the twenties were designed to function in the eighties.

The remaining two restaurants have been inserted into spaces which have little to recommend them to the world of architecture or fantasy. Pearl's in New York City shows what architects of the caliber of Gwathmey-Siegel can do with a shoe box—transform it into a splendid Chinese restaurant where only the food, waiters and Pearl herself are Chinese. For Arby's in Chicago, Stanley Tigerman created a flashy fast food restaurant out of an equally undistinguished space.

All six restaurants have spirit and style—a gift from their architects.

A freshly-cut skylight over the stairwell (left), and a sleek glass brick wall (far left and below) allow natural light to pour through the once-gloomy interior of the old Bear Mountain Inn. Cavernous eating areas were brightened with hanging industrial fixtures and zig-zagging fluorescent strips in the cafeteria (far left), and by circular fixtures with miniature white bulbs in the formal dining room (below left).

George Cserna photos

1
REVIVING THE DINING FACILITIES OF THE HISTORIC BEAR MOUNTAIN INN

The Old Bear Mountain Inn in the Ramapo Mountains of New York had been a landmark for more than three generations. Built in 1914 as a bus terminal and shelter for visitors, the inn had provided eating facilities for 60 years as the focal point of a popular resort that featured swimming, boating, skiing, hiking, and cultural events.

Though the inn's rustic exterior had retained its beautiful Alpine appearance over the years, the building's decaying interior had become a jumble of congested space and dark, gloomy eating areas. Architects Joseph Tonetti & Associates were faced with the task of preserving the inn's historic charm while upgrading dining facilities and lounge areas to handle increasing crowds of visitors to the state park.

Working on a state-allotted budget of approximately $2.1 million, the architects redesigned the building's entrances and exits, and gutted much of the existing interior in pursuit of their two major objectives—to provide better traffic circulation and to get more light into the musty, old inn.

"I enjoy renovation immensely," said architect Tonetti, of the challenge. "Working with an old building is like a puzzle. There are all sorts of things you have to work with and around, and solving the problems is like completing a puzzle."

A major problem was that the building had only one main entrance which opened into a tiny foyer housing the inn's narrow circular stairway. Other exits were rarely used and the main entrance was usually a bottleneck. The problem was solved by removing the circular stairway and creating a large, tiled entry foyer with adjoining hat check area in that space. The architects used a glass brick wall to conceal the downstairs cafeteria just off the foyer, and a wide new stairway to second floor dining and lounge areas was added beyond the foyer. A dramatic 15-by 20-foot skylight was then cut over the stairway to flood the dark center of the building with light.

All building exits and entrances were defined by using custom-made cream and brown awnings for a crisp but subdued effect that blended with the inn's turn-of-the-century flavor.

The only major addition to the inn's exterior was a concrete patio dining area off the inn's west side which was designed to conceal the loading area and garbage bins while offering visitors a tranquil view of Hessian Lake. The patio was furnished with

The only major addition to the inn's well-preserved exterior was a new concrete patio dining area, which conceals loading area and trash bins (left). Preservation was also the primary concern in the inn's main lounge (below). Layers of dirt and old varnish were stripped from the original chestnut ceiling and old chandeliers were repaired. Oak floor and furniture blend with the log-cabin air.

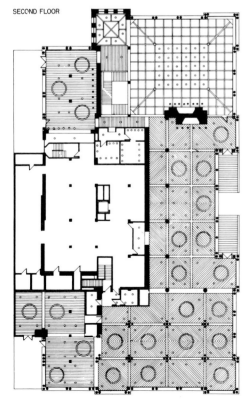

SECOND FLOOR

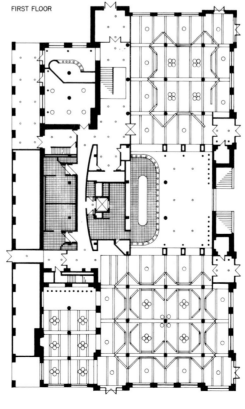

FIRST FLOOR

durable industrial stacking chairs and custom-made tables, with awnings that coordinated with those at entrances and exits.

In the main lounge and dining room on the second level, there was much that, despite decaying appearances, needed to be preserved. "Some of the old-timers were very apprehensive—they hated to see anything at all changed," said Tonetti.

Preserving the lounge's original chestnut ceiling, which was black with dirt and old varnish, the architects stripped and sealed the old wood, and installed unobtrusive linear diffusers for air supply. Quaint old chandeliers were also spruced up by replacing wood parts and cleaning lanterns. An unsightly temporary bar in the lounge was removed, and a handsome new oak bar was constructed in the corner created by moving the original stairwell. Custom-made oak lounge furniture was designed to echo the log-cabin style of the inn.

The old wood floors in the lounge and dining rooms, which were badly deteriorated, were replaced with Appalachian white oak, a material used throughout the inn's renovation for its light color.

In the dining room, drab acoustical tile ceilings were also redone in white oak and mirrored walls and cabinets were used to give the illusion of increased spaciousness and light. The old lighting fixtures in the dining room, which vaguely resembled yellowing parchment paper stretched over a wheel, were replaced by circular fixtures with tiny white bulbs, creating a star-like quality in the dining area at night.

The main dining room was furnished with oak tables that may be covered for formal dinners or used without tablecloths for breakfast and brunch. Caned bentwood chairs were used in the dining room while informal, low-backed oak chairs and bar stools were installed in the smaller Cub Room just off the lounge.

The major portion of the inn's renovation however, was done in the first floor cafeteria. Like the rest of the inn, it needed new plumbing, electrical and mechanical systems and its antiquated food service and storage facilities needed to be replaced. The dismal cafeteria had a low greying canvas ceiling that was hung with old Japanese lantern fixtures. The walls were covered with dark paneling and plaster, and the large eating area was cut into inefficient chunks of space by walls added in an earlier renovation.

The first floor was gutted to expose windows and old stone walls hidden behind dark paneling. A spacious new main entry foyer and stairwell (right, second to bottom) and auxiliary entrances and exits improved traffic circulation, providing more pleasant and efficient dining in the cafeteria (below and top right), the main dining room and the Cub Room (right, second to top).

In an effort to restore as much of the original building as possible, the architects gutted the first floor, exposing and restoring the inn's beautiful old stone walls and arches, and opening the arched windows to let light in. The glass brick wall, which complemented the texture of the stone walls, was used to separate the cafeteria from the foyer.

The old quarry tile floor, a gift of Robert Moses from the 1939-40 New York World's Fair, was still in good shape, and was simply cleaned, patched, and sealed with polyurethane.

Removing several layers of ceiling added in earlier renovations, the architects installed a new pressurized ceiling to increase air circulation while avoiding extensive duct work. The new ceiling was then finished with spray-on acoustical plaster following the structural contours.

Since the first floor cafeteria frequently had to function both as a fast food eating area and as a banquet hall, the new lighting and furniture had to do double duty. The eating areas were given hanging industrial incandescent fixtures for subdued banquet lighting and track lighting was used to wash the stone walls with soft light. Zig-zagging fluorescent strips were used to brighten the area for quick meals during the day.

In the cafeteria, Tonetti chose butcher block tables, and stacking chairs done in oak that lend a more formal look than the chairs used on the patio eating area. Sliding or folding oak doors that disappear into the walls were also installed to curtain off space, separating the enormous cafeteria and dining room into smaller banquet rooms.

Finally, the fast food service area in the cafeteria was enlarged and moved further out into the eating area, permitting more direct traffic circulation from the outside and increasing the efficiency of the service.

Graphics in the eating areas and throughout the lodge were designed to harmonize with furnishings and were later silk-screened and installed by the Park Service.

BEAR MOUNTAIN INN, Bear Mountain, New York. Owner: *The Palisades Interstate Park Commission.* Architect: *Joseph Tonetti & Associates—principal architect: Joseph Tonetti; project architect: Richard Jansen; designer: Rex P. Lalire.* Consultants: *Goldreich, Page & Thropp (structural engineering); Flack & Kurtz (mechanical and electrical engineering); Harry T. Skolodz (food service); The Wolf Company (cost).* Contractors: *Elite Construction Company (construction).*

2
A SPATIALLY COMPLEX AND INTIMATE RESTAURANT WITHIN A LATE-19th-CENTURY MILL

According to the jury's report accompanying a recent award from the Ontario Association of Architects: "The Millcroft Inn in Alton is an outstanding example of the thoroughness, involvement and integrity which architecture should represent." What the jury recognized was the way in which completely contemporary detailing—such as hardware, railings and light fixtures—had been carefully used to enhance, rather than disturb, the atmosphere of the building, built as a mill in 1881. Indeed, a second look reveals that much more than detailing is completely contemporary. For instance, the dining room, a large area, is divided by changes in floor level to achieve greater intimacy. The spaces thus created flow into each other in a very contemporary way, and are modulated by such devices as the overhead lattice-screen wall. Exposed stone walls and old wood decking on the ceiling here seem entirely appropriate, and capitalize on the pastoral waterside setting.

Corridors for access to twenty-two bedrooms on the upper floors surround a new skylighted well that brings natural light to the public rooms below. This whole approach to mixing the best of several eras is accomplished and noteworthy. The inn is part of a $2.5 million-dollar hotel complex on a 100-acre site.

THE MILLCROFT INN, Alton, Ontario, Canada. Architects: *Hamilton Ridgely Bennett—project architect: William Bennett; partner-in-charge-of-interiors: Gordon Ridgely.* Engineers: *Peter Sheffield & Associates* (structural); *Smith Andersen* (mechanical); *ECE Group* (electrical). Landscape architect: *Knecht & Berchtold.* Furniture services: *Elizabeth Geddes Designers Ltd.* General contractor: *E.G.M. Cape Construction Ltd.*

GROUND FLOOR

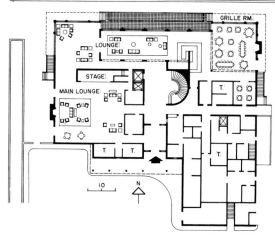

Chuck Ashley photos

3
GENEROUS SPACES FOR YACHT CLUB DINING

The St. Francis Yacht club has been a landmark on San Francisco Bay since it was built in 1928 to designs by Willis Polk. In December 1976 a serious fire destroyed the interiors and a major portion of the walls of the building.

Marquis Associates, approach to the redesign and rebuilding was to preserve the general character of the exterior in massing and materials—barrel tile roofs and stucco walls with arched windows facing the magnificent views of the bay. But on the interior, where a series of alterations had confused the originally simple plan, the architects devised a series of larger more open spaces opening off a clear and generous circulation plan. The lobby is a strong directional space off which the various ground-floor lounges and a small grille room are reached. Along the line of travel, a grand circular stair winds up to the main dining room on the second floor—and here continuous glass walls offer spectacular views of the Bay, and the Golden Gate Bridge. The new furnishings and finishes are bright and appropriate to the club and properly leave any nautical "motif" to the fleet outside .

To minimize the glare common in waterside buildings, Marquis Associates used a long skylight at the rear of the dining room to balance the light; and another skylight in the main lobby brings light into this interior space. A new concrete slab was built on new piles to bring the building into code compliance, and the new structure is steel and wood frame.

SAINT FRANCIS YACHT CLUB, San Francisco, California. Architect: *Marquis Associates—principal-in-charge J. Peter Winkelstein; project architect: Mui Ho; interior designer: Phyllis Martin-Vegue. Engineers: Forell/Elsesser (structural); Gayner Engineers (mechanical); Marion, Cerbatos & Tomasi (electrical); The Engineering Enterprize (lighting); The Marshall Associates (kitchen). General contractor: Plant Brothers Corporation.*

CELLAR LEVEL

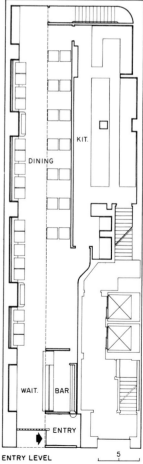

OFFICE

STORAGE

LOUNGE

STORAGE

PREPARATION

REFUSE

KIT.

DINING

WAIT.   BAR

ENTRY

ENTRY LEVEL   5

4
MIRROR TRICKS DOUBLE THE APPARENT SIZE OF A SMALL RESTAURANT

Gwathmey-Siegel was retained when the owner of a well-known restaurant in midtown Manhattan was forced to move to a nearby, but new location. The new space was a 14-foot-wide by 100-foot-deep volume at street level. To counteract these inhospitable proportions, the architects developed a half-vaulted section that reflected in the mirrors over the banquettes, appears to complete itself along the entire length of the space (see photos).

The front elevation reflects the section with surprising accuracy and, in so doing, gives the suggestion that the entire volume was slipped into place.

The kitchen, unexpectedly, runs parallel to the dining area and is linked by a stair to food storage areas in the cellar. A small office, for the owner, is also located downstairs.

The character of the finished interior is elegant, but there is no design overreach. Though the cuisine is Chinese, there is a notable absence of ethnic or thematic decor. The carpet is dark brown, the bar and cabinet work are white oak, the bentwood chairs are cane and white. A combination of wall-mounted and recessed lighting provides enrichment and visual accent without disturbing the restaurant's pleasant, low-key aura.

PEARL's, New York City. Architects *Gwathmey-Siegel—John Chimera, job captain.* Engineers: *Geiger Berger Associates* (structural), *Thomas Polise* (mechanical). Contractor: *All Building Construction Corporation.*

5
SUBURBAN RAILROAD STATION BAGGAGE ROOM TRANSFORMED INTO AN ELEGANT RESTAURANT

While the 19th-century railroad Station at Katonah, New York, scarcely qualifies as landmark architecture, it has, like its more splendid sisters around the country, received the benefit of tender restoration and adaptive use.

At the new Katonah Station Restaurant, the main dining room occupies the old baggage room, where, when travel was more leisurely, luggage was held until it was claimed. Architect Myron Goldfinger retained the utilitarian tongue-and-groove board walls, after sandblasting them to remove half a century's accumulation of paint. He also enlarged the opening into the bar (formerly the waiting room), designing an arched opening to echo existing vaulting and lunette in the area now given to the private dining room (at right in plan).

Because the trains still stop at Katonah—it is a functioning commuter station—it was a condition of the project that the building be open to passengers between 6 and 10 o'clock in the morning. During those hours, tables and chairs are removed from the private dining room and an adjacent alcove; and the banquettes, which Goldfinger fashioned from the old waiting room benches, resume their original purpose. After the commuter rush, the restaurant staff returns the banquette pillows and sets up for lunch.

Restaurant clientele enters through a new door at the front of the building, and is guided by the diagonal bar to the main dining room. Passengers enter the waiting room at the back of the building through a door to the train platform.

KATONAH STATION RESTAURANT, Katonah, New York. Owner: *Ira Marcus*. Architect: *Myron Goldfinger*.

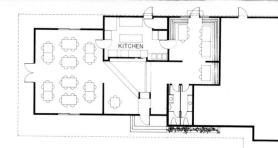

Arby's^R Arby's^R

FAST-FOOD NEED NOT BE SERVED FROM JUNK BUILDINGS

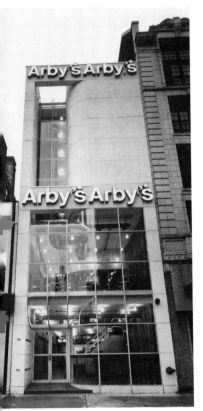

Some conservative Chicagoans must have held their breath when they learned that Stanley Tigerman—an architect whose work nearly always excites admiration and occasionally raises the back hairs of the profession—had been commissioned by Arby's, a fast-food chain, to renovate a four-story commercial building on a highly conspicuous downtown site.

They need not have worried. The design that emerged when the scaffolding came down is inviting, not funky; tasteful, not junky —and decidedly not a bad neighbor (as some had feared) to the historic Water Tower which it faces across Chicago Avenue.

The exterior is infill, stucco and glass, employing both straight-line and curved elements. Behind the glass is a carefully organized fast-food operation on two levels, service below and seating for 90 on the second floor. The two levels are linked by a double stair that breaks up the long narrow volume downstairs. The interior walls are finished in rough-sawn cedar and liberal doses of primary colors are by added color coding air ducts red, lighting tracks yellow, and water piping blue. It is a powerful overhead composition that, coupled with menu boards and other graphics, produces a lively interior, full of invention and fun.

ARBY'S, Chicago, Illinois. Architects: *Stanley Tigerman and Associates*. Engineers: *Raymond Beebe (structural); Wallace & Migdal (mechanical)*. Contractor: *Pepper Construction*.

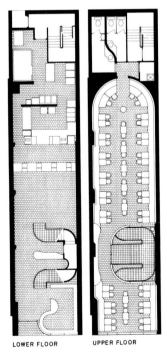

LOWER FLOOR   UPPER FLOOR

7
TRANSFORMATION OF A STREETCAR SYSTEM SUBSTATION INTO A RESTAURANT

This newest Chart House (the same architects have done one on a Boston pier) is in a 1909 building which housed a boiler and substation for Baltimore's streetcar system. It is on a pier in the Inner Harbor, one of the first projects completed in what is to be a major rehabilitation of the area. The exterior of the two-story structure was restored to its original appearance on the two major facades; the harborside facade (which had been bricked in and stuccoed) was given large glass areas to accentuate the spectacular water view from both the dining and lounge areas. An existing masonry bearing wall (see section) became a natural divider between the bar and restaurant. In the bar section (photos this page), a new heavy-timber double truss was designed to support a new mezzanine level and a new roof with a central skylight over the bar—and forms a handsome contemporary foil to the heavy timbers that are so important a part of the interior. The three-level restaurant area (photos opposite) uses the existing floor system, which had remained sound in this portion of the building. A concrete dock on the harborside elevation became a raised seating area; a higher wooden deck inside the front wall of the building was extended back at each side to form a major U-shaped dining level around the central 24-foot-long, stainless-steel broiler bar. The stainless theme is repeated in the round air-handling ducts and the smaller heating/air conditioning ducts throughout the space—a striking counterpoint to the warm wood and brick tones which dominate the space. From this level, stairs lead up to a mezzanine with additional tables overlooking the broiler bar; and in turn, to the third level shown in the plan. Indoor plantings add interest and another appropriate color mass to the spaces.

THE CHART HOUSE, Baltimore, Maryland. Architects: *Anderson Notter Finegold Inc.—Anthony C. Platt, partner-in-charge; Nancy Goodwin, project architect; Jane G. Lucas, interiors.* Engineers: *David M. Berg Inc.* (structural), *Environmental Design Engineers Inc.* (mechanical/electrical). Consultant or historical furniture and antiques: *Charlotte Walters.* General contractor: *Jolly Company, Inc.*

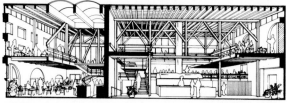

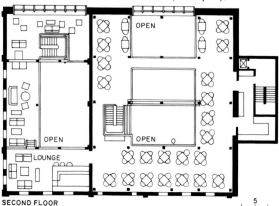

SECOND FLOOR

6

The United States, at least temporarily, has lost the capacity to provide enough new affordable housing to meet the growing demands of its population. Furthermore, what is built today, except for the most well-to-do market, is not nearly as commodious or well constructed as the housing of even the recent past. As a result, we regard more highly our existing housing stock and such buildings as old industrial lofts which can be converted into dwellings. Those who can afford them are eagerly buying up and restoring old houses, sheds, barns, and apartments. "Gentrification" will not solve the housing crisis, of course, and under some circumstances may make it worse, but the efforts of the gentrifiers are often imaginative, ingenious, and artful. The seven examples included in this chapter show what the above qualities, along with money, can do.

In San Francisco, California, a splendid Victorian gingerbread row house was moved 15 blocks to a new site and exquisitely restored. In Chevy Chase, Maryland, architect Hugh Newell Jacobsen stripped an 1870 Victorian house of later accretions, enhanced its 19th-century character by a deft bay window, and added a new wing almost

HOUSES AND APARTMENTS

identical to the old. Not only did he interpretively restore, but he reproduced his own restoration, an eclectic exercise which would have shocked us a decade ago.

The one example from abroad in this chapter is a little villa in Tuscany created from a farm shed. Europeans have been conserving and re-using their old buildings far longer than we, which may account in part for the style and assurance of this remodeling. Another farm building, a Maryland barn, has been remodeled by Moore, Grover Harper. By attaching new wooden exterior walls, the architects have transformed it into a well insulated house which still displays its hand-hewn timber construction inside.

A converted loft building and a single loft remodeling, both in New York City, demonstrate the apartment design opportunities offered by former industrial space. The classically modern Vignelli apartment is located in a Manhattan apartment building of 1909. Like all the examples in this chapter (except for the San Francisco Victorian house, which is a period restoration), the Vignelli work is a fearless juxtaposition of contemporary design within an old and respected setting.

1
A VICTORIAN PAIR

Few readers will recognize Hugh Jacobsen's touch in the exterior of this remodeled Victorian house in a suburb of Washington, D.C. The original portion of this house was built in 1871 as an outbuilding to a larger house of similar style. The main house was long ago erased by a change in the street plan, but the small house remained, surviving several owners and a series of modest alterations.

When the present owner purchased the property in 1975, Hugh Jacobsen was retained to make a new addition and to thoroughly modernize the interiors. But because the neighborhood was old, the corner site prominent, and the Victorian character of the design so lovingly preserved through earlier alterations, Jacobsen carried out the new exterior work using the old mold—or carefully studied reproductions of that mold. The original entry with its covered porch was removed. A floor-to-ceiling bay window was substituted and then repeated on the new wing. Window trim, fenestration and eave details were carefully researched as were paint colors used in small country houses of the 1870s. Both in the old exterior and in the addition, the ethos of the earlier era was preserved, including the promise of well proportioned, carefully developed spaces within.

On the inside, however, the Old Queen would not have found herself at home. The house is fully air conditioned and the interior development of the spaces, their arrangement, their furnishing are pure Jacobsenian. Starting with the glass entry link, and continuing across two floors, the house is contemporary and equipped with all the appurtenances of modern life.

There is always a special feeling about houses in which the old and the new are beautifully harmonized. Here this harmony is achieved very purposefully through a process of historical allusion that, as recently as five years ago, might have been unthinkable for most architects and even today takes courage and sensitivity.

RESIDENTIAL REMODELING, Chevy Chase, Maryland. Architect: *Hugh Newell Jacobsen*. Engineers: *Kraas & Mok* (structural). Contractor: *Owner*.

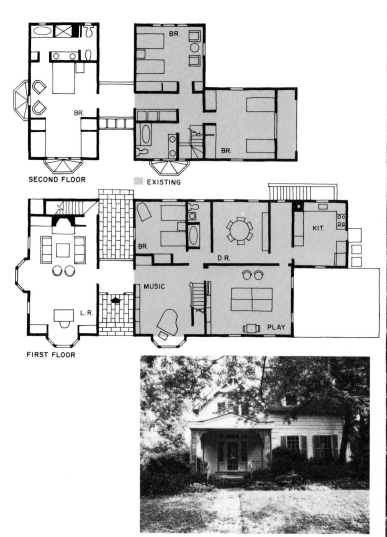

SECOND FLOOR   ▪ EXISTING

FIRST FLOOR

The small photo (above) shows the original portion of the small house. The entrance, across a porch, leads into what is now the music room (photo lower right). The living room (photo below) and bedroom above make up the new addition.

Robert Lautman photos

Just as one test of a design is "can you live with it?", so one test of a designer in his/her own home. Has he gutted the interior, uprooting walls to leave "spaces," or has he sheltered his privacy in conventional rooms? Does he furnish the place with those chairs he designed for Knoll, or does he go for the unimpeachable Barcelona? Does he drink from those cups with the ungrippable handles he designed for Heller, or does he serve those to his guests, himself sipping comfortably from a heavy, chipped china mug?

Many designers turn it all off so they can sleep at night, but Massimo and Lella Vignelli live with their designs round the clock. Their apartment illustrates their talent for composing carefully elaborated settings, frames for variegated action. Yet these interiors are flexible as well as fashionable; stylish, certainly, but not over-stylized.

Even at home, the Vignellis are always designers. They use the apartment for the various scales of entertainment crucial to their careers. Furnished with their designs, their apartment is showroom as well as home.

The design addresses this dual program by compartmentalizing functions. Clearly influenced by the Vignelli's experience in exhibition design, the design of their apartment treats each room as a separate installation, featuring an activity and their designs for it. The design is an analysis of a home, breaking down daily life into component episodes. It seeks to isolate, not integrate, these; to define the parts of this sequence, not to fuse them.

Public and private areas are carefully distinguished. Where the former are hard-edged spaces that preserve all their sharp right angles, the latter are softly outlined and the junction of vertical and horizontal in them is slightly blurred. Where the former clear space around focal objects (a table, a group of couches) the latter tend to push the objects to the edges, leaving the center to be filled by people. Where the public rooms are expanded by real or illusionary vistas opened into adjoining spaces, the private rooms are contracted, turned inward, their windows and doors all but eliminated.

This clear definition of individual *rooms*, each with its own particular character, recognizes the context in which the Vignelli's intervention takes place. In stressing the idea of self-contained volumes, defined by strong walls, the Vignellis have elicited the expressive potential of the massive masonry apartment building. Walls are shown to be thick, ceilings demonstrably heavy. Doors and windows force-

The jewel-like quality of the living room is sharply contrasted in the adjacent library (below). Entered through a narrowing slit of a door (above) that emphasizes the act of passage, the library is a warm, almost womb-like shelter. The Belgian linen which covers the couches, wall, windows and shelves envelops the tranquil, evenly lit room in a soft wrapping. Arranged in symmetrical pairs, standard light fixtures become geometric sculpture.

The dining room, which opens off the rear of the living room and, via a small passage, off the library, is a space whose austere bareness throws the objects it contains into sharper relief. Originally a plain box, with a small fireplace on one wall and the Vignelli's assemblable Quattro Cilindi table in the center, it has been transformed into an elegant dining hall by the insertion of two mirrors flanking the protruding fireplace. By elongating perceived space, the mirrors confer dignity on what is actually a relatively simple room, adding an element of sophisticated ambiguity and intrigue to the space (above, Massimo Vignelli in the dining room).

LOWER LEVEL

UPPER LEVEL

fully violate these dense, solid cases in punching through them. The emphasized weight of the shell plays it up as a "found object," an old carapace invested with new activity.

This evocation and transformation of the defining qualities of the existing building describes, in a subtle layering of contrasts and comparisons, both the modernity of the Vignelli's design and its simultaneous classicality. The light beige walls, naked save for baseboard and molding, the carpetless light wood floors, throw into high relief the pure geometry of the furniture (mostly the Vignelli's earlier, more severe work). At the same time, the sand finish of those walls and the parquet fitting of the floor, sanded so that every peg and plank shows, heightens the presence, the density of the structural divisions by emphasizing their texture.

Furnishings and furniture delve into the material of which they are made in a similar fashion. The library, for example, mines possible meanings of natural-colored Belgian linen in the seating, wall, and window coverings. The Quattro Cilindi table at its center takes wood as its subject; the door-sized plank lies on log-shaped cylinders—or can be fitted into their ends so that they become columns, the plank a roof. The object changes form in response to its context; the low table is sunk into the pillowy library, while the high version is erected amid the perpendicular planes of the dining room.

We, too, moving from room to room, respond to this alternation of hard and soft, open and closed, public and private, void and solid, positive and negative. The strictly maintained duality establishes, as it were, two axes in terms of which our motion is plotted and invited.

One of the Vignelli's early posters for the Museum of Modern Art, New York, states in two dimensions what their apartment states in four. In this poster, heavy black horizontal lines carry the information, while vertical separations group it into categories. Through the center, in gravity-defying stopped motion, leaps Fred Astaire, clicking his heels at the top of his hyperbolic trajectory. Human activity sparks geometry. In the Vignelli's apartment, as in their work, it is we (or the Vignellis) who activate the design by moving within it, providing the curve that gives the encompassing grid direction and meaning.

VIGNELLI APARTMENT, New York, New York. Architects: *Massimo and Lella Vignelli.* Lighting consultant: *Howard Brandston.* Contractor: *John LaBarca.*

The intimacy of the library (above) is intensified in the master bedroom (below). Here Belgian linen pads even the ceiling, cabinets, and window (as a heavy drapery). A few crisp-edged black, Vignelli-designed objects—the Saratoga bed (1970), the Metaphora I table (1979) maintain the horizontal and vertical lines.

The guest room (above), a linen tent, was created out of a garret. In their son Luca's room (below) carpeted, stepped platforms forming sleeping and sitting areas are punctuated by a huge "column" anchoring the end of a partition. The cylinder, which marks the entrance to the bath, contains a shower.

4
A VICTORIAN RESCUED—AND
RAISED TO LANDMARK QUALITY

The renaissance of what has been dubbed "Victoriana" throughout the West Coast means more than just fresh paint and new windows. It is, rather, a preservation attempt exemplified by this Victorian house.

The house was designed in the Stick Eastlake style in 1876 by Samuel and Joseph Newsom, well-known California-based architects who were prolific designers of housing. It had fallen into disrepair, as had its entire neighborhood. An energetic San Francisco Redevelopment Agency years ago designated this area as Western Addition and with the aid of Federal monies had begun rejuvenation. In one spot where demolition was slated, several structurally sound houses, including this Victorian, were sold to the highest bidders under the condition that each be moved to a new site. George Stewart bought this Newsom-designed house, and it was moved 15 blocks to a new site with all the nervousness and tenseness to be expected. It was blocked up, raised onto a flat-bed truck and maneuvered through the streets like a turtle, with crews of men removing and then replacing overhead telephone and power lines. While the two sites were similar, the second was slightly narrower and so the house had to be "squeezed" into place on a 25-foot-wide lot, cutting off a quarter inch of a side bay window. Only the first and second floors were moved; at the

Rob Super photos

SECOND

FIRST

GROUND

second site a new foundation had been prepared and the two floors were positioned atop a garage and a newly designed rear apartment. An unusual high tower at roof height was removed and rebuilt later.

Architects Susan Bragstad of the Redevelopment Agency and Peters, Clayberg & Caulfield collaborated on the restoration and remodeling. Meticulous attention was given to the restoration of the classic ornate facade with its profusion of ornamention. Characteristic of the Newsom brothers' designs, the exterior form is dominated by square bay windows crowned with a tower.

After the house had been rehabilitated, it was then recognized and placed on the National Register of Historic Places and chosen by the San Francisco Landmarks Preservation Advisory Board as one of the most important Victorian structures in the City. It has also been designated the theme logo building for The Foundation for San Francisco's Architectural Heritage.

STEWART RESIDENCE, San Francisco, California. Owner: *George E. L. Stewart.* Architects: *Peters, Clayberg & Caulfield* and *Susan Bragstad of the San Francisco Redevelopment Agency.* Structural engineer: *Nishkian, Hammill & Associates.* Landscape architect: *Max A. Schardt.* Interiors consultant: *Cliff J. Hines.* General contractor: *Rosenmayr Development Co.*

The Stewart residence is a combination of restoration and remodeling, totaling 4000 square feet. Because there had been many owners and nearly as many remodelings of the interiors, care was taken to restore special elements, including tracking down the original bannister which had been stolen when the house sat idle. A unique double back-to-back stairway, separated by its original screen, leads to the second floor. On the ground level, a separate rental apartment was added behind the garage, with its own private entrance and access to a rear deck and garden. On the first floor, the formal living and dining rooms (see previous pages) were retained and restored, but an open kitchen (top right), informal dining area and porch (left), and greenhouse (top left) were added. In order to replace deteriorated or missing sections of moldings and trim, the plasterer made molds on site, and later in his workshop extruded new pieces from plaster or plastic.

5
A MID-19th-CENTURY BARN RECYCLED INTO AN ENERGY-EFFICIENT HOUSE

The owners of this old barn placed some unusual constraints on the architects they commissioned to convert it to a second home. Certain of the constraints, in addition, seemed in a sense to conflict. The owners wanted the renovation to be energy-efficient, for instance, but they also wanted the original siding and roofing to be retained and remain visible from within. They wanted the first-floor structure of stone walls (circa 1850) and hand-hewn timbers to be celebrated, but they also wanted the barn highly receptive to the sun.

To accomplish these priorities, the architects begn by building new exterior walls, fastening them by means of ledger strips to the old plates. New rough siding was also applied and left to weather. Because the old rafters could not support another layer of roofing, the architects nailed 2x6s through the existing metal roof into the rafters creating a "T" section that would support new horizontal members and a new metal roof. The cavity this created was filled with insulation.

Along its south wall, the old barn had been built with an integral shed. But the shed cut off long views to the Choptank River as well as winter sunlight, so the architects stripped it of its siding, removed sections of its roof and in this manner created a trellised structure (photo right) that adds enormously to the character of the renovation.

Five solar collectors on the south-facing section of the roof provide domestic hot water, while a conventional oil burner is used for space heating. When the house is unoccupied, the two systems are set in tandem and the thermostat set way down.

"We worked hard," says Mark Simon, "to retain and even enhance the rough-hewn character and yawning openness that makes this building a barn, while at the same time giving attention to special places where the inhabitants live and play."

A marvelous renovation.

BARN RENOVATION, Eastern Shore, Maryland. Architect: *Moore, Grover, Harper*—*project architects: Charles Moore and Mark Simon.* Engineer: *Ronald Schaeffer* (structural). Interiors: *Samuel Marrow.* Landscape architect: *Lester Collins.* Contractor: *L.G.R., Inc.*

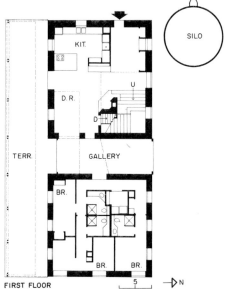

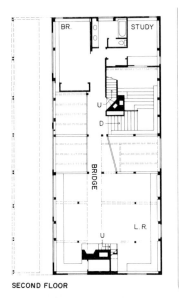

FIRST FLOOR 5 →N

SECOND FLOOR

Norman McGrath photos

The major spaces are distributed over three levels or partial levels. The entry is on the west wall and leads to a small vestibule. From here, the view leads to a broad staircase that passes behind a stucco-covered chimney up to the second-floor living room. A second flight of steps leads to the third floor. As the photos eloquently show, all the major spaces are anticipated through a tantalizing fretwork of beams, posts and braces. Wherever possible, the architects have retained details and hardware from the earlier era—the wood bolt on the door (previous page) being a fine example.

6
TRANSFORMATION OF OFFICE TOWER TO APARTMENTS CREATES LUXURIOUS LIVING SPACE

Bill Rothschild photos except as noted

The renovation of a New York City office building into apartments has not only given a boost to inner-city housing but has done so in a luxurious manner, providing a quality of living space that can be an inducement for people to stay or move into the center city. Even though the building was not originally designed as an apartment complex, it can seriously compete with other luxury housing in the city because of its design amenities.

Constructed in 1929, this 24-story office building, located near the United Nations on Manhattan's East Side, was severely damaged by a gas explosion in 1974. The explosion funneled up the elevator shafts on the west side, blowing out a 50-foot-wide section of the brick facade from the street level to the top story, but structural damage was confined to the bank of elevators. The architects converted the service elevators to passenger use and cut away the demolished shafts and bent steel frame, leaving a V-shaped end wall (right). This provides a small street level courtyard and opens up the full 200-foot height of the west wall of apartments to natural light. This change also decreased the building's total volume, and zoning regulations permitted this "lost" space to be regained in the form of greenhouse-type windows installed on the exterior of most upper floors above the 17th level.

The interiors were designed to capitalize on views, light and spatial variety. A total of 341 apartments benefit from the commercial proportions of the building—12-foot-high ceilings, and 8-foot-high windows running the width of most apartments.

The addition of greenhouses to the exterior is a major aspect of this conversion of office building to apartments. Each glass enclosure extends the apartment outward onto the terrace, and visually highlights the linear apartment design.

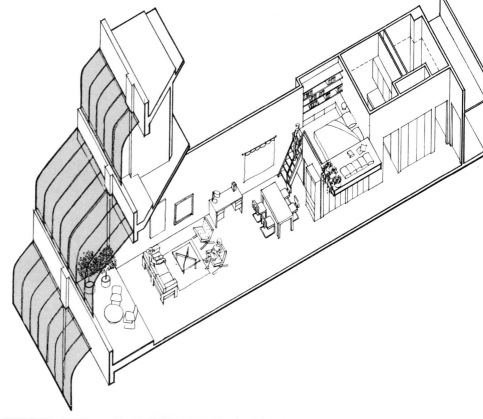

An example of the creative utilization of the structure's idiosyncrasies is the redesign of the service elevators for passenger use. Because the cab platforms were larger than permitted by building codes, a glass-enclosed terrarium was located in the rear of each, providing an unexpected, yet pleasing experience.

The building's entrance was formerly the truck loading dock. Now multi-leveled (with a barrier-free access ramp) connecting a 100-foot-long lobby with elevators and street level entrance, it has been designed in a modern idiom but reminiscent of the building's 1929 origin.

The project is the largest carried out so far under New York City's J-51 tax abatement program, which provides tax incentives for the conversion of commercial properties into residential use (explained in detail on page 111). It also has turned a serious disaster into a very successful asset.

TURTLE BAY TOWERS, New York, New York. Owner: *Rockrose Development Corporation.* Architects: *Bernard Rothzeid & Partners—Peter Thomson,* partner-in-charge; *Bernard Rothzeid and Carmi Bee,* project designers; *Vinod Devgan,* job captain. Engineers: *Harwood and Gould* (structural); *George Langer* (mechanical/electrical). Consultants: *Ranger Farrell Associates* (acoustical); *Nathan Silberman* (codes); *Soloman Sheer* (Board of Standard Appeals). Interior design: *Bernard Rothzeid & Partners— Marjorie Colt.* General contractor: *Rockrose Construction Corporation.*

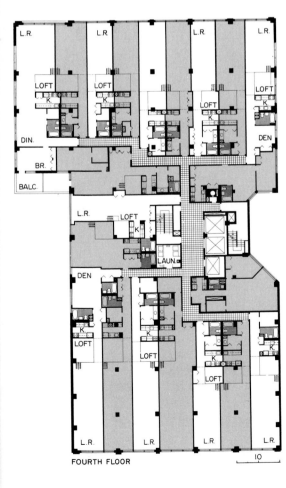

TENTH FLOOR

Lofts were included in the design of many apartments, especially studios, for they provide a spatial variety to the predominantly linear units. There are 341 apartments on the half-acre site, with configurations varying from studios to "townhouses" on the upper floors.

PENTHOUSE (LOWER FLOOR)

PENTHOUSE (UPPER FLOOR)

FOURTH FLOOR

10

Susan Schwartz

7
LOFT LIVING: BIG SPACES, FRESH IMAGES

At the time of purchase, this five-story loft building—a former cord factory—in Lower Manhattan showed many of the signs of neglect that make this kind of building economically attractive and certain design idiocyncracies that might be turned into architectural virtues. The floors were in poor condition and needed patching. The stamped tin ceiling, nailed right to the wood joists, was in sad disrepair. Transverse partitions, some of them awkwardly positioned with respect to the structural grid of heavy timber, chopped up the space wastefully. In addition, all the mechani-

5

cal and plumbing services were at one end of the 25- by 90-foot floors.

The architect/owner Alan Buchsbaum removed the partitions and made repairs to finish. He opened the space to its full length. In plan, he zoned out the principal functions, being guided by obvious requirements for light and privacy. The kitchen, needing large amounts of neither, was placed near the center of one of the long walls. But to bring the services to it from the rear wall, the bedroom and dining areas had to be raised up to create a false floor. Across from the

kitchen, Buchsbaum set up a work area with drafting tables, tack space and supply cabinets. The plan is completed by living space and bedroom at opposite ends.

In general feeling, the loft is casual and unselfconscious, although sculptural accents—as at the long kitchen counter—betray an abiding concern for form. Most of the furnishings are simple, informal, and selected for their potential for easy rearrangement. Buchsbaum has gotten considerable design mileage from subtle contrasts in textures.

The bedroom however, presents a somewhat different vocabulary of form and finish—a vocabulary of more studied elegance and more dramatic contrasts. The raised floor is finished in a smooth, high glaze, off-white tile that turns up at the built-in bed to form an enclosure for the mattress. The closet has mirror-glass doors and the whole space is defined in the long axis by a gently undulating glass block partition that slaloms leisurely around a pair of heavy wood columns. The lighting is subdued in the bedroom although the glass block partition is actually lighted from both sides. A row of airport fixtures, floor mounted with rigid conduit and fitted with blue bulbs, lends the space an unexpected trace of mystery.

The building has three owners (Buchsbaum is one) and each occupies a floor. To put the project on a sounder economic footing, the remaining space has been turned into rental property.

LOFT FOR ALAN BUCHSBAUM, New York City. Architects: *Alan Buchsbaum and Stephen Tilly.* Lighting design: *Paul Marantz.*

The raised platform—required for plumbing—provides carpeted seating for the dining table which is set in a circular cutout. Over the dining area (photo at right) is a tapestry/sculpture executed in felt and designed by Robert Morris. The bath, with its open shower, is shown reflected (photo below). It is finished, like the bedroom, in reflective materials.